Civil War Sites
in Virginia
A
TOUR
GUIDE

Civil War Sites

James I. Robertson, Jr.

University Press of Virginia

in Virginia

A TOUR GUIDE

Charlottesville

THE UNIVERSITY PRESS OF VIRGINIA
Copyright © 1982 by the Rector and Visitors
of the University of Virginia

Sixth printing 1996

Library of Congress Cataloging in Publication Data
Robertson, James I.
  Civil War sites in Virginia.

  Includes index.
  1. Historic sites—Virginia—Guide-books. 2. Virginia—Descrip-
tion and travel—1951-   —Guide-books. 3. Virginia—History—
Civil War, 1861–1865. I. Title.
F227.R59   917.55'0443   81-7426
ISBN 0-8139-0907-4   AACR2

Printed in the United States of America

Contents

Preface

No state contributed more to the Southern Confederacy, or suffered more from the Civil War, than did Virginia. The Old Dominion had traditionally been a leader of the American experiment in democracy. Beginning as a haven of patriots, Virginia became a producer of presidents. Its statesmen held front-rank positions in every decade during the United States's first half-century. Virginia possessed a prestige that the embryonic Southern nation sorely needed.

Prestige was only a part of what Virginia had to offer. Its borders stretched from the Atlantic Ocean to the Ohio River. Washington, D.C., the national capital, was literally a next-door neighbor. Over 1,047,000 residents made Virginia the most populous of Southern states. Its resources included a rich diversity of mineral deposits, harbors, farmlands, and livestock. Virginia's capital, Richmond, was the most industrialized city south of Philadelphia. The Confederate States of America would not have lasted four years had not Virginia given so much of itself to the Southern cause.

The Old Dominion was one of the last states to leave the Union. Yet because it was the most exposed geographically of the seceding states, Virginia became the major battleground of the Civil War. The bitterest and bloodiest fighting in the history of the Western Hemisphere took place in a narrow band of land extending from Manassas to Petersburg. Thousands of Americans were killed, and tens of thousands more were wounded or captured, as fields and woods became sanctified by the blood of Northerners and Southerners who were tragically fighting for the same thing: America, as each side interpreted what the American nation should be.

That the Confederacy survived during 1861–65, that the war raged without resolution for four long years, was attributable in large measure to the military leadership furnished by Virginia. Any list of generals begins almost invariably with Robert E. Lee. As commander of the Army of Northern Virginia, he had responsibility for the defense of most of the state. Lee proved to be a veritable genius at strategic maneuver as he shifted attention away from the Southern capital at Richmond. Not until two years after Lee assumed command—in 1864, when Confederate forces were in a state of irreversible deterioration—was a Federal army able to advance any distance south of the Rapidan River.

By April 1865, however, Virginia lay prostrate. It had borne more combat and absorbed more bloodshed than any other single state. Twenty-six major battles, more than 400 smaller engagements, plus the years of maneuvering by opposing armies, had wrought widespread destruction. Northern Virginia lay in ruins. The Shenandoah Valley had been systematically destroyed. All of Fredericksburg and much of Richmond were in ashes. Petersburg was pockmarked from bombardments. Norfolk and the Hampton Roads naval works were in shambles. Countless farms and homes were charred skeletons of past splendor.

Then there was the human toll. Eighteen Virginia generals were among the more than 17,000 sons of the Old Dominion who had perished in battle or died from sickness. No way exists to measure the full impact of such a loss.

Virginia was also the only state in the Civil War to lose territory as a direct result of hostilities. A third of the Old Dominion broke away and, in 1863, became a separate state.

Today Virginia is vibrant, diverse, and progressive. It thinks of the present and plans for the future. Yet Virginia also remembers the past, more so perhaps than most states. To begin to forget, to fold away years gone by, Virginians first had to recall and pay tribute.

This the state has done to a commendable degree. Hundreds of monuments dot the land. The many preserved battlefields are quiet now, with only the wind disturbing areas where the blood of patriots merged. The graves of Civil War soldiers have the aura of shrines. In the 1930s Virginia became the first state in the nation to establish official highway historical markers, and the project continues still. Today more than 460 of those markers provide on-site information about Civil War events and participants.

Until now, no concerted effort has ever been made to catalog all of the major Civil War attractions in the Old Dominion. This book seeks to meet that need by providing data on and directions to every site of significance. Most of the monuments and markers were erected in the years before the construction of the interstate highway system. Visitors must therefore proceed on national and state roads when in quest of historical reminders.

In Virginia, the number of extant Civil War buildings is so high that certain restrictions had to be established for inclusion here. Buildings and homes which have been appreciably altered over the years so that they bear little resemblance to their wartime appearance have been omitted. Private homes, for the most part, are cited only when the current owners have expressed willingness to have visitors inspect the grounds. On the lawn of almost every county courthouse in the state is a monument of some kind to Confederate soldiers from that area. Included in this tour guide are only those of unique design and those bearing useful lists of names.

Many Civil War points of interest in Virginia are victims of time and nature. Fort Sedgwick, a key point in the 1864–65 siege of Petersburg, is now the site of an automobile service station. Where Libby Prison stood in Richmond is a parking lot. Rattlesnakes, bats, and lack of lighting make three wartime saltpeter mines in Wise County too dangerous to visit. On the other hand, here for the first time is a guide to scores of visitable Civil War attractions.

To organize the sites and facilitate tours, this book divides Virginia into six geographic sections. Descriptions of Civil War scenes in each section are code-numbered on maps to correspond with numbers affixed to each locale or site in the narrative. Each summary also contains specific directions for reaching that attraction via today's highways.

Unless otherwise noted, all sites mentioned here are free of charge.

Many of the scenes of yesteryear have a symbolism that reawakens a common patriotism. In a small cemetery at Appomattox, eighteen soldier-graves stand in a row. Seventeen of them contain Confederate soldiers; the grave at the end is that of a Federal soldier. They sleep side by side, and it is fitting that they do; for these American heroes who lived not so long ago struggled greatly against something greater than themselves. Often fighting for nothing more than the realization of a dream, they bravely marched down the undiscovered road to tomorrow. What they gave, we now share. What they lost, we gained. Their sacrifice is the nation's legacy.

I am genuinely grateful to scores of persons who responded in writing to inquiries about historic sites in every community of the state. Particularly am I indebted to the following friends who shared their love of Civil War history by giving me personal tours of scenes in their locales: Ernest C. Clark, Glade Spring; John E. Divine, Waterford; Robert C. Freis, Culpeper; Emory L. Hamilton, Wise; Kim Bernard Holien, Alexandria; Robert K. Krick, Fredericksburg; John V. Quarstein, Newport News; and Dabney W. Watts, Winchester.

The J. Ambler Johnston Research Fund of the VPI Educational Foundation made it possible for me to crisscross the state several times in order to examine historic sites. I shall always be inspired by "Uncle Ambler" Johnston and the lifelong love for Virginia that he possessed.

My wife Libba first pointed out the need for such a study. She gave constant encouragement (as well as some prodding) throughout the various stages of compilation, and she was a valuable companion on research trips through the Old Dominion. In many ways, this is her book.

JAMES I. ROBERTSON, JR.

Virginia Polytechnic Institute
and State University

Civil War Sites in Virginia

A
TOUR
GUIDE

THE BATTLE OF WINCHESTER

Northwestern Virginia

The Shenandoah Valley (also known as the Valley of Virginia) extends southwestward from the Potomac River to Lexington. Its grainfields and large orchards made it "the bread basket of the Confederacy," and the region was a principal source of supplies for Lee's Army of Northern Virginia during much of the war. In addition, the Valley was a veritable lifeline for both North and South. Lying between the two easternmost ranges of the Appalachian Mountains, leading northward as well as southward, it was also like a dagger pointed at the western flank of the Union and Confederate armies. Neither side could advance safely and far into enemy territory unless it had security in the Shenandoah Valley. This explains why the region was the scene of major campaigns in 1862 and again in 1864. All told, some 112 engagements were fought within its narrow confines.

In the early 1960s the Virginia Civil War Commission erected ten pairs of "Circle Tour" markers at the sites of the major battles. The concept was to enable tourists to make a circular tour between Winchester and Harrisonburg via U.S. 11 and U.S. 340. These signs are excellent visual aids to the principal engagements in the Valley.

Northwestern Virginia

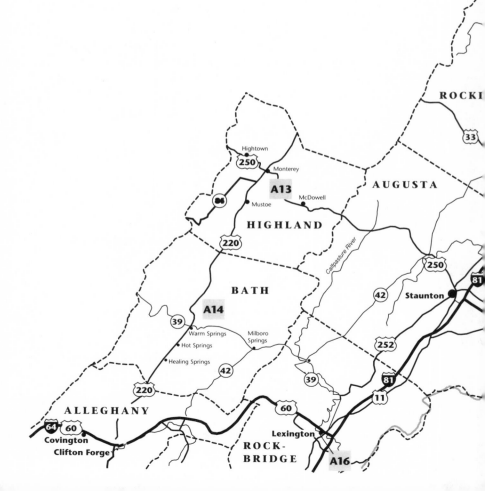

A1 WINCHESTER Once called "the gateway to the Shenandoah Valley," Winchester was the most strategic point in the 135-mile Shenandoah corridor. As a result, it became the scene of more warfare than any other town west of Richmond. Winchester changed hands 72 times during the war. It contained as many as six military hospitals. Commanding generals on both sides used it for a headquarters. By war's end, the community was a battered shell of what it once had been.

Major Battlefields Four major engagements were fought in and around the city: Kernstown (March 23, 1862), First Winchester (May 25, 1862), Second Winchester—or Stephenson's Depot (June 14–15, 1863), and Third Winchester—or Opequon Creek (September 19, 1864). No traces of any of the battlegrounds remain for visitors. In the 2100, 2700, and 3000 blocks of Valley Lane (U.S. 11 South)—all on the west side of the highway—are markers commemorating the 1862 battles. Circle Tour signs for Second and Third Winchester are located on the west side of U.S. 11 at the northern edge of town.

Jackson's Headquarters During November 1861–March 1862, Gen. Thomas J. ("Stonewall") Jackson had his headquarters in a French-style home that is now a museum. Many Jackson memorabilia are on display. Admission charge.

The home is at 415 N. Braddock Street, one block west of the downtown's Loudoun Street Mall.

Confederate Monument Dedicated in 1916 and restored in 1979, the memorial depicts in bronze a young Virginia infantryman departing for war.

The statue is located in Loudoun Street Mall, in front of the county courthouse.

Sheridan's Headquarters   Federal Gen. Philip H. Sheridan directed operations in the 1864 second Valley campaign from an imposing home on the southwest corner of Braddock and Piccadilly streets. It was from here, on October 19, 1864, that Sheridan began his famous ride to rally the crumbling Union army under attack at Cedar Creek. The home is now the Elk's Club and not open to the general public.

Stonewall Cemetery   Some 3,000 identified Confederate soldiers are interred here. In addition, a tall stone shaft in the center of the cemetery honors 829 unknown Southern troops killed in the fighting around Winchester. The obelisk, dedicated in 1866, is among the earliest Civil War monuments. General Turner Ashby, Jackson's cavalry chief, is one of the notables buried here.

Boscawen Street runs east from downtown and leads into Mount Hebron Cemetery, of which the Confederate burial ground is a part.

National Cemetery   Here lie 2,110 known and 2,381 unknown Federals who died in the Winchester campaigns. This is one of the largest national cemeteries in Virginia. It is across Woodstock Lane from Stonewall Cemetery.

Entrenchments   On U.S. 522 South, 3 miles from Winchester and on the north side of the highway, can be seen earthworks constructed in 1863 by Federals occupying the town. These remains are on private property.

A2   CEDAR CREEK   The last-ditch Confederate attempt here to dislodge Federals from the Valley was a dramatic battle of might-have-beens. At dawn on October 19, 1864, Gen. Jubal A. Early's Southern army delivered a heavy surprise attack that soon had two Federal corps on the verge of rout. Ragged and starving Confederates then began falling out of action in order to loot abandoned camps. Federal Gen. Sheridan had just reached Winchester after a conference in Washington. Sheridan quickly mounted his horse, raced to the battlefield, and rallied his forces. "Affairs at times looked badly," he reported, "but by the gallantry of our brave officers and men, disaster has been converted into a splendid victory." Cedar Creek was the last major battle fought for control of the Shenandoah Valley.

Today several highway markers pinpoint the undeveloped and unencumbered battle site. It lies a half-mile south of Middletown alongside U.S. 11. Take Exit 77 from I-81.

Belle Grove Situated in the center of the Cedar Creek battlefield, this mansion was completed in 1794. James and Dolley Madison spent their honeymoon here. In the autumn of 1864 Sheridan used the home as headquarters. It now houses a museum that is open during April–October. Admission charge.

A3 FRONT ROYAL This seat of Warren County was chartered in 1788 and initially known as "Hell Town." The city became a base for Belle Boyd, a teenager who was an accomplished spy on behalf of Confederate efforts in the Valley. On May 23, 1862, Stonewall Jackson's men stormed the Union garrison here and captured 750 of 1,000 Federals.

Warren Rifles Confederate Museum Included in the displays are memorabilia relative to Miss Boyd, Lee, Jackson, Early, Ashby, and other Confederate leaders, plus artifacts of the war in the Valley. The museum is open from mid-April to November. Admission charge.

This exhibit is at 95 Chester Street in the downtown area.

Soldiers' Circle Monument Located in Prospect Hill Cemetery, this memorial stands over the graves of 276 Confederate dead.

Mosby Monument Also in Prospect Hill Cemetery, this monument is flanked by two Parrott rifled cannon. The stone commemorates seven members of Mosby's Rangers who were illegally executed as spies by Federals at Front Royal in the autumn of 1864.

Battle of Front Royal Monument This bronze plaque atop a stone base summarizes the May 1862 engagement. It is at the intersection of Royal Avenue and Chester Street.

A4 THOROUGHFARE GAP One of the major passes through the Blue Ridge Mountains, this area was of vital importance to both sides. The Confederate troops of Gens. Stonewall Jackson and James Longstreet used this pass in the flanking movement that produced smashing victory in the August 1862 battle of Second Manassas.

Thoroughfare Gap is 6.8 miles west of the intersection of Virginia 55 and U.S. 29.

A5 STRASBURG This village had strategic value during the war because of its location at the northern base of Massanutten Mountain, which divides the Shenandoah Valley in half for fifty miles. Signal Knob, on the northern face of the Massanutten, was used by both armies to spot troop movements. It still dominates the eastern skyline.

Fisher's Hill   On September 22, 1864, occurred a late-afternoon battle in which Sheridan's overwhelming numbers inflicted a second major defeat on the Confederates in three days. The Southern army lost 1,400 men. Among the dead was Col. A. S. ("Sandie") Pendleton, who had been one of Jackson's favorite officers.

Circle Tour signs denote the site of the battle 2 miles south of Strasburg on U.S. 11.

Hupp's Hill   Remains of trenches thrown up by Federals in 1864 can be seen 1 mile north of Strasburg along the west side of U.S. 11.

A6   EDINBURG   For a month in 1862 this town was the base of operations for Gen. Turner Ashby's Southern cavalry. Some 28 skirmishes took place in the vicinity during that period. In October 1864 Federals began a systematic destruction of the Valley known as "The Burning." Sheridan ordered the grain mills at Edinburg set afire. When two young women of the town appealed tearfully to Sheridan to spare the mills because they were Edinburg's only livelihood, the general ordered the flames extinguished. The Edinburg Mill still stands today.

Exit 71 off I-81 leads into Edinburg.

A7   MOUNT JACKSON   This was an important wartime locale because it was the western terminus of the Manassas Gap Railroad, one of only two lines connecting the Shenandoah Valley with the rest of Virginia. The bridge at the south edge of town was burned by Federals in their retreat following the 1864 battle of New Market. Just north of downtown, on the west side of U.S.

11, is an obelisk marking the graves of 112 unknown Confederate soldiers.

Mount Jackson is reached by taking Exit 69 off I-81.

A8   NEW MARKET   One of the most dramatic battles of the Civil War took place here. On May 15, 1864, a Federal army advancing to destroy the railroad at Staunton met a hodgepodge force of Confederates that included 257 teenage cadets from the Virginia Military Institute. The outnumbered Southerners attacked in a drizzly rain and, after severe fighting, overran the Union lines. Today the finest Civil War museum in the state is on this battlefield. Displays, dioramas, artifacts, movies, and a walking tour are some of the attractions. Admission charge.

Leave I-81 at Exit 67. The battlefield park is on the west side of the interstate.

Circle Tour markers of this engagement are 1.1 miles north of New Market on U.S. 11. Two hundred yards north of those signs is a monument to a Pennsylvania regiment which suffered 45 percent casualties in that battle.

A9   LACEY SPRING   Some maps will denote this spot as Lincoln Spring, for it was here that the ancestors of Abraham Lincoln first settled. Immediately northwest of the present village, on an elevation a quarter-mile west of U.S. 11, is a cemetery containing many of the sixteenth president's forebears.

Lacey Spring is between Exits 65 and 66 off I-81, on parallel U.S. 11.

A10   HARRISONBURG   Located at the southern tip of Massanutten Mountain, Harrisonburg had an additional military value as a vital road junction. Stonewall Jackson used the town as a rendezvous point several times during the 1862 Valley campaign.

Electric Map   A large electrified relief map, along with a 27-minute narration, provides an excellent overview of the 1862 battles for control of the Shenandoah. Admission charge.

The map is at the Harrisonburg–Rockingham County Historical Society, 301 S. Main Street.

Battle of Harrisonburg   On June 6, 1862, two regiments of Confederates attacked a Federal regiment; and in the ensuing fight for control of Chestnut Hill, Gen. Turner Ashby was killed. Descriptive markers and a monument at the site of Ashby's death are at the field.

From Exit 63 on I-81, proceed 0.5 mile southeastward on County 659. Turn left on County 1003 for 0.4 mile. The markers are on the right.

A11   CROSS KEYS   Here and at nearby Port Republic is where the 1862 Valley campaign ended. In the second week of June, Jackson found himself between two approaching Federal armies. The Confederate general divided his smaller force to meet the dual threat. Federals under Gen. John C. Frémont marched out of Harrisonburg and on June 8 attacked part of Jackson's waiting army under Gen. Richard S. Ewell. A furious Southern counterattack inflicted almost 700 losses on Frémont's forces before they abandoned the field. The countryside today remains basically as it looked at the time of the battle.

Take Exit 63 (County 659) from I-81 southeastward for 7.2 miles. A bronze tablet on the north side of the road identifies the battleground. In addition, a Circle Tour set of highway markers on Virginia 276 a few hundred yards south of County 659 graphically describes the action.

A12 PORT REPUBLIC On the day following Cross Keys occurred the climactic engagement of the 1862 campaign. Confederates under the personal command of Jackson assailed converging Federals along the eastern bank of the Shenandoah River. The Southerners were eventually victorious, but at a heavier cost in men. The battlefield now is relatively unmarked by progress.

From Exit 63 (County 659) off I-81, drive 11.5 miles southeastward to the intersection with U.S. 340. Turn left—north—on U.S. 340 for 1.1 miles to Circle Tour markers, situated at a spot where the entire Port Republic battleground is clearly visible. Inside the village of Port Republic is also a useful roadside battle map.

A13 McDOWELL On May 8, 1862, the second major battle of the Valley campaign exploded when Jackson arrived here seemingly from nowhere and confronted a Federal army advancing eastward through the mountains. Fighting lasted five hours. At midnight the Federals used campfires to mask their retreat from the area. Today the hills constituting Jackson's right flank are conspicuous from the highway; while the battlefield itself is virtually intact, it is all on private property. Two roadside markers pay tribute to the engagement. Inside the village—0.9 mile west of the battleground—stands the McDowell Presbyterian Church, which was one of the buildings used as a hospital during and after the fighting.

At Exit 57 on I-81, take U.S. 250 west through Staunton for 35.1 miles. The picturesque highway snakes over four mountain ranges. On the mountaintop at the Augusta-Highland county line are remnants of Confederate entrenchments dug in the first year of the war.

A14   BATH COUNTY   Although at the remote western edge of the state, Bath County boasts several Civil War attractions. The area is best reached east-to-west by Virginia 39 and north-to-south by U.S. 220. This is mountainous country, where slow driving is imperative.

Millboro Springs   Just south of this mountainous village, on the right-hand (west) side of County 633, are remains of entrenchments and gun emplacements. Their origins are unknown.

Bath Alum Springs   Located 6.5 miles west of Millboro Springs on Virginia 39, this was a favorite wartime resort for soldiers and civilians. Only a few trees remain to show where the shaded driveway existed. During the winters of 1861–62 and 1863–64, Confederate cavalry camped in the fields north of the highway.

Warm Springs   This well-known spa, 6.5 miles west of Bath Alum Springs, was a focal point for this area of the state during the war. The Warm Springs Hotel (no longer standing) served as a hospital and headquarters for both sides. The wartime courthouse is now an inn. The wife and children of Gen. Robert E. Lee spent much of the war here. In the Ladies' Bath House is a chair especially made for the arthritically crippled Mrs. Lee.

Flag Rock   This promontory was a signal post used by Confederates and Federals alike during the conflict.

Proceed 3 miles east of Warm Springs on Virginia 39 to the top of Warm Springs Mountain. Flag Rock is visible to the south.

A15 WAYNESBORO On March 2, 1865, Federal cavalry under Sheridan broke Early's Confederate lines here and captured most of the town's 1,000 defenders. This engagement was the last major contest fought for control of western Virginia.

Harman Monument This simple stone marker stands at the spot where Col. William H. Harman died in the battle of Waynesboro. Harman, a resident of Waynesboro, had served from 1851 to 1863 as Commonwealth's attorney for the county.

The marker, as well as a highway historical sign, are on U.S. 250, 0.1 mile west of the intersection with U.S. 340.

Confederate Monument In Riverview Cemetery is an obelisk honoring some of the Southern troops who died at Waynesboro. Names from four states are listed on the shaft.

Riverview Cemetery is on U.S. 340 at the first stoplight south of the junction of U.S. 340 and U.S. 250.

A16 LEXINGTON No town of its size in Virginia contains more historical attractions. Lexington was the home of wartime governor John Letcher. It was the site of Virginia Military Institute, the South's premier military academy. So wedded to the Southern cause were Lexington's citizens that the tiny community sent an artillery battery and an infantry company into service. On June 10, 1864, Federal troops entered Lexington and burned a substantial portion of the town, including VMI buildings.

The town is accessible via Exits 51-53 off I-81.

Jackson Home The only residence that Stonewall Jackson ever owned served as his home during his 10-year tenure as a VMI professor. The building has been restored and furnished to appear as it looked during Jackson's stay there in the 1850s. Admission charge.

The home is situated at 8 E. Washington Street, one block east of Main Street and across the street from the county courthouse.

Stonewall Jackson Cemetery Here lie the remains of Jackson, members of his family, and a number of the town's leading statesmen and soldiers. Some 400 Confederate soldiers are said to be buried in the cemetery.

The burial ground is in the 300 block of S. Main Street.

Washington and Lee University Robert E. Lee served as the college's president in the five years immediately after the Civil War. The center of attraction on the campus is the Lee Memorial Chapel. The remains of Lee and most of his family are entombed here. Edward Valentine's recumbent statue of Lee is alone worth the trip to Lexington. In the basement of the chapel is a museum of college mementos, with emphasis on Lee's contributions.

Proceed one block west of Main Street on Henry Street to the visitor parking lot beside the chapel.

Virginia Military Institute Since its establishment in 1839, this school has been one of the leading military academies in the Western Hemisphere. It contributed a host of officers and men to the Confederate cause. In the center of the campus is an unusual statue depicting Stonewall Jackson standing in the wind. Nearby are original cannon from the famous Rockbridge Artillery. On the east side of the parade ground stands Sir Moses Ezekiel's seated statue of *Virginia Mourning Her Dead*, a monument to the cadets who fell in the 1864 battle of New Market. An on-campus museum provides an excellent summary of VMI's heritage.

The academy is north of and adjacent to Washington and Lee University. North Main Street passes to the east of the parade ground.

North Central Virginia

The Piedmont region of Virginia lies between the flat coastal lands to the east and imposing mountains to the west. It is an area composed of gently rolling hills, small clumps of trees, and beautiful vistas. In 1860 fences of stone and rail were dividers between orchards, grain-fields, and vast pasture lands. Communities were small and scattered, thereby making communication tenuous at best. The northern Piedmont thus became ideal for cavalry operations; and in the last two years of the war, a Virginia horseman so dominated activities in the region that it was often called "Mosby's Confederacy."

No area of the state suffered more in the Civil War than did north central Virginia. Scores of small engagements, streams of wounded men, hordes of stragglers from both armies, destruction of crops, and looting of homes were regular scourges. Little clothing, less food, no medicines, and sleepless concern over loved ones serving in Lee's army were other tribulations suffered by residents of this area. They felt the angry hand of the Civil War for almost the entirety of its four years. The occupations and counteroccupations by opposing armies ultimately gave the section another name: "The Desolate Land."

North Central Virginia

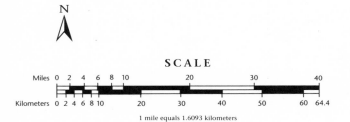

N

SCALE

Miles   0   2   4   6   8   10   20   30   40

Kilometers   0   2   4   6   8   10   20   30   40   50   60   64.4

1 mile equals 1.6093 kilometers

ALBEMARLE

29

20

2

Charlottesville   B14

250

29

6

6

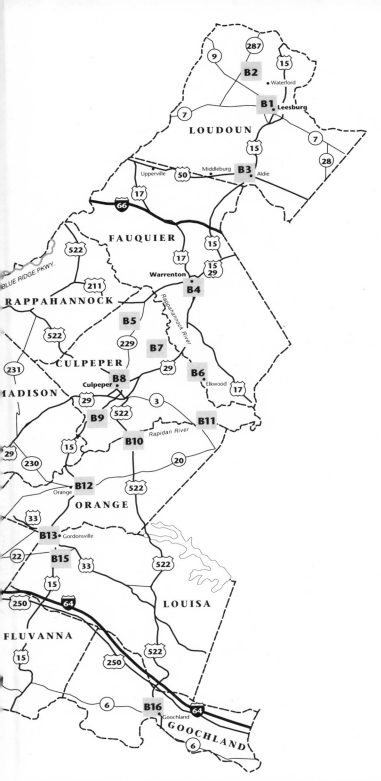

B1 LEESBURG   This was a focal point in northern Virginia for both armies. Lee shook down his forces here in September 1862 before launching the first invasion of the North. General Lewis A. Armistead of Gettysburg fame served as provost marshal of Leesburg for a time. The town is also associated with the exploits of Col. John S. Mosby, the legendary "Gray Ghost of the Confederacy." A number of wartime homes remain standing, but all are privately owned.

Loudoun Museum   This small depository, at 16 W. Loudoun Street, is in a vintage-1850s building and displays a number of Civil War artifacts.

Ball's Bluff   Here occurred one of the first Union disasters of the war. When a Federal force of 1,000 men crossed the Potomac River on an October 1861 reconnaissance, Southern reinforcements rushed to the threatened area and drove the bluecoats back over the bluffs to the river's edge. Scores of Billy Yankees died from musketry from above; others drowned, their bodies floating slowly downriver to Washington. A small but impressive national cemetery and stone markers to two heroes in the fighting are on the battlefield today.

From Virginia 7 at Leesburg, go north on U.S. 15 Bypass for 1.9 miles. Turn right on the unnumbered dirt road for 1 mile to the dead end and battle site.

B2 WATERFORD   In the center of this history-filled village is the Waterford Baptist Church, scene of a shoot-out more characteristic of the American West. On August 27, 1862, a company of Federal cavalry took cover in the church when confronted by an equal number of Confederate troopers. The ensuing gun battle left the front of the brick structure pockmarked with bullets, which are quite visible still.

Waterford is 4 miles west of Leesburg via County 662. The church is at the intersection of County 665 and 783.

B3 ALDIE Aldie, Middleburg, and Upperville were witness to bitter mounted engagements during June 17–21, 1863. Total losses were higher than those incurred subsequently by cavalry at Gettysburg. George A. Custer, William W. Averell, and Elon J. Farnsworth were all Federal junior officers in these engagements; yet a week later, all three had been elevated to the rank of brigadier general. The only memento of the three battles is a monument to the 1st Massachusetts Cavalry. One of its captains, Charles Francis Adams, Jr., wrote of Aldie: "My poor men were just slaughtered and all we could do was to stand still and be shot down."

From U.S. 50 at Aldie, turn north on County 734 for 1.3 miles to the monument at the top of the hill.

B4 WARRENTON This city was under Federal control for most of the war. It was the target of several raids by Mosby's partisan rangers. All but two of the town's churches were used as Union hospitals. Saint James Episcopal Church was left unharmed so that one place for worship by all denominations would be available. On the other hand, the Presbyterian church was converted into a stable. Warrenton contributed three companies to the Confederate armies. The most noted of those units was the "Black Horse Cavalry," whose war record earned it the title of "The Bravest of the Brave."

Old Court House The present building, constructed after a fire in the 1890s, is an almost exact replica of the wartime courthouse. Among the portraits gracing the walls inside are likenesses of several Civil War figures from Fauquier County. A monument to Mosby stands on the courthouse lawn.

The building is at the downtown crossroads where Warrenton began.

Warren Green Hotel This was a commodious nineteenth-century hostelry. From the upper porch, in November 1862, Gen. George B. McClellan delivered his farewell address to the Federal Army of the Potomac that he had created. The building now houses county offices.

This renovated structure is on Hotel Street in downtown Warrenton.

Mosby Home Built around 1850, this is one of the most beautiful homes in the city. It became the postwar residence first of Col. Mosby and then of Gen. Eppa Hunton, who commanded a brigade in Pickett's Charge at Gettysburg. The home is privately owned.

Mosby's residence is at 173 Main Street.

Marr House This clapboard dwelling, also in private possession, was the residence of Capt. John Q. Marr of the "Warrenton Rifles." Killed in action on June 1, 1861, Marr is regarded as the first Civil War battle fatality in Virginia.

His home is at 118 Culpeper Street.

Warrenton Cemetery A tall shaft dominates this burial ground and marks the resting place of Col. John S. Mosby. Some 600 unknown Confederate soldiers are interred here.

The cemetery is on Lee Street, within walking distance of the downtown.

B5 LITTLE FORK CHURCH   At this Episcopal church Company D ("The Little Fork Rangers") of the 4th Virginia Cavalry Regiment was organized. The troopers used the church grounds as a drill field before departing for war. A unique stone monument to this company stands behind the church.

This site, midway between Warrenton and Culpepper, is reached via Virginia 229 and County 624.

B6 KELLY'S FORD   Only two markers call attention to the March 17, 1863, fight here. Opposing cavalry brigades fought a running battle over brush-covered terrain. One of those killed in the action was the youthful but inspiring Maj. John Pelham, who commanded Stuart's Horse Artillery. Three months earlier at Fredericksburg, Lee had praised the Alabamian as "the gallant Pelham."

Just south of the Rappahannock River crossing of U.S. 15-29 is Elkwood. In the front yard of a home at the intersection with County 685 is a weather-beaten monument to Pelham's memory. A few yards north of this intersection is the junction of U.S. 15-29 with eastbound County 674. Approximately 4 miles down the county road is Kelly's Ford itself. Deep in the woods (a path now exists) is a tiny marker supposedly pinpointing the spot where Pelham was leading men forward when he was struck by a shell fragment. Some historians dispute this site.

B7 BRANDY STATION   Often termed "the greatest cavalry battle ever fought on American soil," this June 9, 1863, engagement raged for 11 hours and extended over fields and through woods. The Confederates managed to retain the field; but in almost all other respects, the battle was a victory for Federal horsemen—their first major success of the war. The battlefield today is virtually unchanged from its 1863 appearance. Two historical markers grace Fleetwood Hill, the key point in the fighting.

Brandy Station is 2.1 miles south of Elkwood on U.S. 15-29 and 5 miles north of Culpeper. At the junction with County 663, turn west to ascend Fleetwood Hill. It is visible a few hundred yards from the main highway.

B8 CULPEPER The town of Culpeper was one of the most important points in Civil War Virginia. It was a railhead on the Orange and Alexandria Railroad; Robert E. Lee's army used it repeatedly for bivouac and encampment; Federal Gen. Ulysses S. Grant commandeered the hotel for his headquarters before the 1864 campaign; and many of the town's churches, homes, and commercial buildings became hospitals for soldiers wounded in nearby battles.

Cavalry Museum   This small but impressive exhibit includes a 30-minute slide program on Culpeper's role in the war. The presentation fully explains why the city is sometimes called the "Cavalry Capital of the Civil War."

The museum is part of the Chamber of Commerce offices at 102 N. Main Street.

National Cemetery   The majority of Union soldiers in this rather large burial plot succumbed to illnesses such as pneumonia and typhoid fever.

From the downtown area, proceed 3 blocks east of Main Street to the cemetery entrance.

Fairview Cemetery   In this principal cemetery for Culpeper stands a monument to a mass grave of Confederates, most of whom are unknown.

This cemetery is 5 blocks west of Main Street on U.S. 522.

Redwood   John Strother Pendleton, one of Culpeper County's most influential wartime citizens, lived in this imposing mansion. Generals Lee and Longstreet met several times at Redwood; Gen. Jeb Stuart was a houseguest there; and it is believed that Maj. Pelham spent the night there before his death the following day at Kelly's Ford. The estate is privately owned, but the grounds may be visited.

From Main Street in Culpeper, take U.S 522 (Sperryville Pike) for 1.2 miles. Turn left at the sign on the south side of the highway.

B9   CEDAR MOUNTAIN   On August 9, 1862, in rolling country south of Culpeper, Confederates under Stonewall Jackson collided with the van of Gen. John Pope's advancing Union army. Federal regiments attacked on both sides of the highway. Jackson's line barely held until reinforcements arrived and turned the battle in the South's favor. The area today is as close to its wartime appearance as any battlefield in Virginia.

A state highway marker denotes the battle site 5.1 miles south of Culpeper on U.S. 15.

B10 CLARK MOUNTAIN Here was a vital signal station for Confederate armies for much of the war. From its heights Jackson and Lee both observed Pope's movements before the Second Manassas campaign. On May 2, 1864, Lee stood atop the mountain and watched the beginning of Grant's advance into the Wilderness. The eminence still offers one of the most panoramic views of the Virginia Piedmont.

As one travels south on U.S. 522 from Culpeper, the mountain will become increasingly conspicuous on the west side of the road. Just after crossing the Rapidan River, turn right (west) on a paved road marked by a Moormont Orchards sign. The road curls up to the mountaintop.

B11 GERMANNA FORD This site was a heavily used crossing of the oftentimes imposing Rapidan River. Three times during the war (April 30 and November 26, 1863, and May 4, 1864) the Federal Army of the Potomac waded over the river here to launch offensives against Lee's forces.

Virginia 3 crosses the Rapidan precisely at Germanna Ford.

B12 ORANGE Although this county seat was never witness to a major engagement, a number of skirmishes occurred near it. The town became a favorite rendezvous point for the Confederate Army of Northern Virginia.

Courthouse Architecturally, the courthouse looks as it did in wartime. Local units used the basement of the building for an arsenal in the conflict's first weeks.

The courthouse is in the center of town, on U.S. 15.

Saint Thomas's Episcopal Church This is the only surviving church in the area that reflects Thomas Jefferson's architectural tastes. In 1863 President Jefferson Davis, Gens. Lee, A. P. Hill, and William N. Pendleton, and other army notables all attended services here. The pew where Davis and Lee prayed is marked. According to local legend, Lee hitched his horse, Traveller, to a locust tree that still stands in front of the church.

U.S. 15 ascends a hill just south of downtown Orange. Saint Thomas's is on the crest of the hill, a half-block south of the point where U.S. 15 makes a ninety-degree turn.

B13 GORDONSVILLE The junction here of the Virginia Central and the Orange and Alexandria railroads made this village one of the strategically vital areas in north central Virginia. Gordonsville became a major supply depot; Confederate forces encamped here regularly; one of Virginia's larger military hospitals operated here for the last three years of the conflict.

Exchange Hotel Originally constructed as an overnight accommodation for railroad travelers, this three-storied building became the central structure for the Gordonsville Receiving Hospital. It is now being restored and, when completed, will house a museum of the Civil War period.

This gray and yellow building is on U.S. 33 at the eastern edge of the downtown area.

Presbyterian Church   The church's beginnings go back to the 1840s. The sanctuary maintains its wartime appearance. One of the most beloved of Confederate ministers, Daniel B. Ewing, was pastor of the church. A plaque notes that Gen. Stonewall Jackson worshiped here several times in 1862.

The church is on U.S. 33 between the downtown and the traffic circle junction with U.S. 15.

Maplewood Cemetery   Nearly 700 Confederate soldiers died at the receiving hospital. Temporarily buried behind the Exchange Hotel, the bodies were later reinterred in the local cemetery. Headstones were not placed over the individual graves. Today the remains lie in a grassy plot surrounded on three sides by woods, with a bronze marker denoting the burial ground.

From the traffic circle of U.S. 15 and 33, continue west on U.S. 33 for 0.6 mile. Turn right into the cemetery, continue straight until the semipaved road makes a ninety-degree curve to the left. Proceed another 20 yards. The plot and marker are on the right.

B14   CHARLOTTESVILLE   This city was known during the war primarily for its military hospitals. Federal troops seized and occupied Charlottesville in 1864.

University Cemetery   The remains of 1,200 Confederate soldiers, most of whom perished from sickness, lie here. Centerpiece of this burial ground is a bronze statue of a bareheaded Confederate soldier.

The cemetery is located at the northeast corner of Alderman and McCormick roads, just north of the University of Virginia football stadium.

Lee Statue   Completed in 1924, this equestrian statue was the work of sculptors H. M. Schrady (who died while the project was underway) and Leo Lentelli.

The monument is in a small park 2 blocks north of the Downtown Mall, between 1st and 2d streets.

Jackson Statue   This most impressive monument was the creation of Charles Keck and antedates the Lee statue by three years. The Jackson memorial is unique in that it depicts the general bareheaded and galloping forward on his beloved mount, Little Sorrel.

The statue is 3 blocks north of the Downtown Mall, on 4th Street.

B15   TREVILIAN STATION   Cavalry under Sheridan were moving westward in an attempt to establish a link between Grant's army at Richmond and Federal forces at Charlottesville. On June 11, 1864, troopers under George A. Custer attacked the Confederates of Wade Hampton and Fitzhugh Lee. The fighting was confused and indecisive. The following day, Sheridan renewed the assaults without success. In the two-day engagement, combined losses exceeded 1,700 men. Today a bronze plaque (dedicated by the United Daughters of the Confederacy) and a highway historical tablet call attention to the site of the first day's action.

The markers are 200 yards east of the junction of U.S. 33 and Virginia 22, on the south side of the highway.

B16   GOOCHLAND COUNTY

Goochland County Jail   This building, erected in 1825, served as a Federal prison in the latter part of the Civil War. In March 1865 Union cavalrymen liberated the inmates, then burned the building. Legend has it that a Pennsylvania captain prevented his men from setting fire to the nearby courthouse as well because he thought that the deeds needed to be preserved to prove ownership of land.

The jail is on Virginia 6 in the county seat of Goochland.

Dover Steam Mill Ruins   During the war this grinding mill was a two-storied structure with arched voids. On March 1, 1864, Federal raiders under Col. Ulric Dahlgren burned the mill.

Ruins of the mill are on private property. From Virginia 6, proceed north on County 642 for 0.2 mile.

Pleasants Monument   A stone marker honors James Pleasants, a county Confederate hero who reputedly captured 13 Federals and killed another.

From Goochland, drive west on Virginia 6 to County 670; turn right to the intersection with County 641. The monument is at this juncture.

THE BATTLE OF CEDAR MOUNTAIN — VIEW FROM THE UNION LINES.

SUPPER AFTER A HARD MARCH.

COBB'S AND KERSHAW'S TROOPS BEHIND THE STONE WALL.

Northeastern Virginia

On a map it looked so easy. The two opposing capitals, Richmond and Washington, lay only 110 miles apart. All the numerically superior Federal armies seemingly had to do was to lunge forward across the Potomac and make a four-day march southward. Seize Richmond and the South's political core—as well as its leading industrial city—would be lost and the war would be over. Yet Confederate military leaders were optimistically aware that a southward advance on Richmond would be costly for any invader. If Confederate shore batteries or naval vessels could keep Union gunboats out of Virginia's large rivers, and if Southern troops could control the few mountain passes through the Blue Ridge, the distance and terrain between the capitals offered the South an almost ideal defense.

Dense forests, broad rivers running west-to-east, and swampy areas were natural barriers to any move on Richmond from the north. Further impeding a Union advance was the vital rail junction at Manassas. Any movement from Washington had first to be southwest to the junction so as to protect the Union flank, then southeast toward Richmond. An expeditious Confederate general might choose his battleground and strike at any point in the narrow 100-mile-wide corridor between the mountains and the Chesapeake Bay. As long as the opposing armies bore any relation to each other in size, the Northern battle cry of "On to Richmond!" could be a siren's song, lulling Federal brigades onto a killing ground.

And a killing ground northeastern Virginia tragically became.

Northeastern Virginia

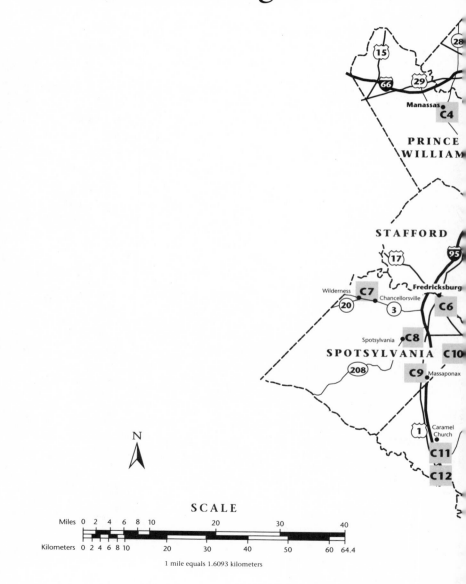

28
15
66
29
Manassas
C4

PRINCE
WILLIAM

STAFFORD

17
95

Wilderness
C7
Fredricksburg
Chancellorsville
20
3
C6

Spotsylvania
C8

SPOTSYLVANIA
C10

208
C9
Massaponax

1
Caramel
Church

C11

C12

N

SCALE

| Miles | 0 | 2 | 4 | 6 | 8 | 10 | | 20 | | 30 | | 40 |

| Kilometers | 0 | 2 | 4 | 6 | 8 | 10 | 20 | 30 | 40 | 50 | 60 | 64.4 |

1 mile equals 1.6093 kilometers

C1 ALEXANDRIA This important river port was situated directly across the Potomac from the Northern capital. Hence, Alexandria became vulnerable from the moment of Virginia's secession from the Union. The city dispatched four companies into Confederate service before its May 1861 occupation. Being safe behind the lines for the remainder of the war enabled Alexandria to escape destruction. Yet its use as a Federal supply base, hospital depot, and port of embarkation drastically altered its prewar appearance.

Fort Ward One of 68 forts and batteries that formed a defensive circle around Washington, Fort Ward stood on a commanding eminence and boasted 36 gun emplacements. The northwest bastion of the fort has been reconstructed, with renovations made to other portions of the works. The headquarters building contains numerous artifacts and displays. In many respects, this is the most attractive Civil War site in the greater Washington area.

The fort is at 4301 W. Braddock Road, which lies between Virginia 7 and Seminary Road west of downtown Alexandria.

Ivy Hill Cemetery Here can be seen the graves of Frank Stringfellow, a noted scout for Gen. Jeb Stuart, and C.S. Navy Capt. Sidney Smith Lee.

From Fort Ward, proceed 1.7 miles east on King Street (Virginia 7). Ivy Hill Cemetery is on the north side of the highway.

Alexandria National Cemetery First begun in 1862, this burial ground contains the bodies of more than 3,750 Union soldiers. Also to be found here are the graves of four civilians who assisted in—and died during—the pursuit of Lincoln assassin John Wilkes Booth.

This national cemetery is at Wilkes and Payne streets in the downtown area.

17th Virginia Infantry Monument   Most of Alexandria's fighting men joined the 17th Virginia Infantry Regiment. This monument, located in the middle of the city's main street, marks the spot where the first volunteers formed to march off to meet a Federal threat at a place called Manassas.

The stone obelisk is at Washington and Prince streets.

Christ Church   One of the most famous Episcopal churches in Virginia, this building dates back to colonial days. Robert E. Lee was confirmed here; and it is asserted that on April 21, 1861, following morning services, Lee met with representatives of Gov. John Letcher, who tendered him command of all of Virginia's military forces. In the graveyard behind the church are the remains of the South's ranking general, Samuel Cooper, and Confederate diplomat James Murray Mason. A mass grave of Confederate dead is also located here.

Two blocks north of the 17th Virginia monument, at Washington and Cameron streets, stands Christ Church.

Stabler-Leadbetter Apothecary Store   A metal plaque on the outside wall explains that here, in October 1859, Lt. Jeb Stuart handed a message from the secretary of war to U.S. Army Col. Robert E. Lee directing Lee to proceed at once to quell a disturbance by John Brown at Harper's Ferry.

The apothecary is at 105 S. Fairfax Street, four blocks east of Washington Street.

Boyhood Home of Robert E. Lee   Here the future Confederate general spent much of his boyhood. The home, built in 1795, is lavishly furnished with early nineteenth-century pieces. Admission charge.

From Washington Street, go a half-block on Oronoco to No. 607.

C2   ARLINGTON   Since 1965, Arlington County has erected 52 historical markers to indicate the sites of Civil War forts, hospitals, and other notable buildings. Fragmentary remains of a few of the forts still survive on private properties; yet the growth of the Washington suburban area has taken a deadly toll of the scenes of yesteryear.

Arlington National Cemetery   This is understandably the most famous of the federally administered cemeteries. Eighty-one Union generals lie buried here, as well as Robert Todd Lincoln and Confederate Gen. Joseph Wheeler. One monument stands over the mass grave of 2,111 Federal dead. Sprinkled throughout Arlington are special Congressional Medal of Honor gravestones. (This highest of American awards originated during the Civil War.) At Jackson Circle, near the rear of the cemetery, are 250 Confederate soldier-graves. In their midst is an impressive bronze monument created by noted sculptor Sir Moses Ezekiel, who lies buried nearby.

The visitor center for Arlington National Cemetery is at the base of the hill at the south end of Arlington Memorial Bridge. Individual auto tours of the cemetery are not permitted. Tourmobiles traverse the area on a regular schedule. Rider fee.

Custis-Lee Mansion   George Washington's stepgrandson built this home on an estate that is now Arlington National Cemetery. In 1831 Robert E. Lee married Mary Randolph Custis inside the Greek Revival mansion, and the couple made their home there for thirty years before the war.

Visits to the home are part of any tour of the national cemetery.

Fort Myers Established in 1863, this is the only remaining defense of the Northern capital still in use. Stationed here is the 1st Battle Group, 3d Infantry Regiment, which provides guard details for Arlington National Cemetery and acts as honor guard for funerals of presidents and other dignitaries.

The main entrances to this installation are on U.S. 50, immediately behind the national cemetery.

C3   FAIRFAX COUNTY This is a large and increasingly metropolitan area which nevertheless contains a number of varied Civil War sites. Unfortunately, they are scattered throughout the county. The attractions below are listed in a sequence whereby the visitor will travel roughly in an arc west from Arlington and ending near the southern outskirts of Alexandria. However, to make this swing will require a driver's patience through always-heavy traffic.

Fort Marcy Another anchor in the wartime defenses of Washington, this site is now operated by the National Park Service. It is presently in a natural state, with interlinking earthworks visible for several hundred yards. Interpretive markers, cannon, and a picnic area are at this overlook on the Potomac River.

The fort is located on the north side of the George

Washington Memorial Parkway, just east of the McLean exits.

Freedom Hill Fort   Off the beaten path here is an excellent example of a Civil War redoubt. This fortified picket enclosure was designed for 100 men and was used to guard Federal camps from raids by such Confederate units as Mosby's Rangers. The interpretive markers are unique and outstanding.

Take Virginia 123 south toward Vienna. Two-tenths of a mile south of the intersection with Virginia 7, turn right (north) on Old Court House Road for 0.3 mile. Freedom Hill Fort is on the left.

Fairfax Courthouse   This was a famous building seen often in Matthew Brady photographs of the war period. It was used as a signal post and headquarters building throughout the Civil War.

The courthouse stands in downtown Fairfax at the intersection of Virginia 123 and 236.

Marr Monument   Located on the grounds of the courthouse, this stone marker pays tribute to Capt. John Q. Marr, killed early in the war at that spot. The two boat howitzers flanking the monument were captured by Confederates at the battle of First Manassas.

Mosby's Capture of Stoughton   In a daring midnight raid on March 8–9, 1863, Capt. John S. Mosby and 30 Virginia troopers galloped into Fairfax. Federal Gen. Edwin Stoughton was taken prisoner as he lay ignominiously asleep in bed. The small band of Southerners also seized 32 other Federals, 58 horses, plus arms and equipment. This performance first called attention to Mosby's potential as a partisan ranger.

A monument to the midnight raid stands 2 blocks west of Fairfax Courthouse on Virginia 236 (Little River Turnpike). Behind the monument is the Truro Parish House, where Stoughton was spending the night. It is now privately owned.

Confederate Cemetery Monument Large markers denote the graves of known and unknown Confederate dead. During the Civil War, the cemetery was the site of a Union stockade.

From Fairfax Courthouse, proceed 4 blocks west on Virginia 236, then turn left into the cemetery.

Saint Mary's Church This simple Catholic church, in a picturesque setting, was where Clara Barton (founder of the American Red Cross) tended scores of wounded Federal soldiers during the 1862 Second Manassas campaign. The field between the church and the railroad became an outdoor ward for innumerable injured soldiers.

Continue south on Virginia 123 from Fairfax Courthouse for approximately 3 miles. Turn right on Fairfax Station Road, 0.2 mile before crossing the Southern Railway overpass. The church is visible from Virginia 123.

Pohick Church Completed in 1774, Pohick Church was for decades a familiar landmark in the northern Virginia area. George Fairfax, George Washington, and George Mason served as vestrymen. During the Civil War, the church was in a sort of no-man's land, and it suffered extensive damage—including much carving of initials on the soft sandstone walls. The graffiti are quite visible today.

When Virginia 123 terminates at I-95, proceed north

on the interstate to Lorton Road. Exit there and go east to the dead end, then left (north) on U.S. 1 for 1 mile. The church is on the right.

U.S. Army Engineer Museum Like all armed services museums, this one has exhibits pertaining to the full scope of American military history. Some displays treat of engineering matters in the 1860s.

The museum is inside Fort Belvoir at 16th Street and Belvoir Road. Entrances to the fort are along U.S. 1 north of Pohick Church.

Fort Willard This property, recently acquired by the Fairfax County Park System, offers a superb example of an earthen fortification in an unimproved state. Fort Willard was another of the 68 forts that encircle Washington. It provides a beautiful view of the Potomac River. Although situated now in a residential area, the site will undergo restoration in the near future.

If traveling north from Pohick Church, continue 9.5 miles up U.S. 1 to Beacon Hill Road. (A shopping center is on the west side of the intersection.) Go east on Beacon Hill Road for 1.1 miles to a stoplight, then left on Fort Hunt Road for 0.5 mile. Turn left again, this time on Glen Drive. Proceed 0.2 mile, bearing left at the fork near the top of the hill. The road will circle around the site of Fort Willard.

C4   MANASSAS Railroads from the south and west merged at Manassas and made the junction a point of major importance to both sides. Who controlled the railhead in essence controlled northern Virginia. On a hot Sunday in July 1861, the first major land battle of the Civil War took place here. The fighting forces were more akin to armed mobs than to armies. That the battle lasted the better part of a day and was marked by courage and determination on both sides was a tribute to Americans as a whole. In the Confederate victory, Gen. Thomas J. Jackson gained his nickname, "Stonewall."

Thirteen months later, on much of the same ground, occurred the battle of Second Manassas (or Second Bull Run, as Northerners called it). Jackson was instrumental in holding Gen. John Pope's army at bay until Lee arrived to drive the Federals from the field. Three days of combat produced almost 24,000 casualties. This smashing Confederate success cleared the way for Lee's first invasion of the North.

ON THE WAY TO MANASSAS. A VIRGINIA SCENE IN '61.

Manassas National Battlefield Park The National Park Service has done a commendable job in maintaining portions of the two battlegrounds. A visitor center, displays, and guides are available to the public. The equestrian statue of Jackson atop Henry House Hill is a moving sight.

At the 47-mile marker on I-66, turn north on Virginia 234. The NPS visitor center entrance is between I-66 and U.S. 29.

Manassas Museum Open only in the afternoons, this display presents a history of the rail-junction town. The emphasis, of course, is on the war years. Admission charge.

The museum is at 9405 Main Street in downtown Manassas.

C5 STRATFORD HALL This birthplace of Robert E. Lee stands on a cliff high above the Potomac River. The home has been restored and holds many furnishings of the Lee family. Admission charge.

Proceed 40 miles from downtown Fredericksburg east on Virginia 3 to the junction with Virginia 214. Turn left and continue 1.1 miles to the estate.

C6 FREDERICKSBURG Situated at the falls of and at a critical bend in the Rappahannock River, Fredericksburg had been a chief river port for the Shenandoah Valley since colonial times. Two major battles were fought within its limits, and the town changed hands no less than seven times during the war.

Battlefields The first large-scale struggle for control of the city occurred on a cold Saturday in December 1862 when Federals made more than a dozen assaults against Lee's strong entrenchments. Fighting raged until nightfall. The result bordered on a massacre and prompted Lee to state during the battle: "It is well that war is so terrible; else we should grow too fond of it." Losses in the Army of the Potomac exceeded 12,000 men; Confederate casualties were less than half that number.

In May 1863, as part of the Chancellorsville campaign (see C7), Union troops again attacked Marye's Heights at Fredericksburg. This time they were successful in driving the Southerners from their works.

The starting point for touring these sites is the National Park Service visitor center. It is located on the battlefields at the base of Marye's Heights, on which some 15,000 Federal soldiers are now buried. Available at the NPS center are a new slide-movie, exhibits, and guided tours. A 7-mile drive on an NPS road provides an almost-constant view of Confederate trenches as well as a better understanding of the extraordinary length of the 1862 battle line.

From I-95, take Virginia 3 east for 1.3 miles. Turn right near the bottom of the hill onto Sunken Road and proceed for 2 blocks. The visitor center and parking lot are on the left.

Confederate Cemetery Established in 1865 by the Fredericksburg Ladies Memorial Association, this burial plot contains the graves of 2,000 Southern soldiers (only 330 of whom have been identified). In this relatively small cemetery lie the remains of six Confederate generals: Seth M. Barton, Dabney H. Maury, Abner M. Perrin, Daniel Ruggles, Henry H. Sibley, and C. L. Stevenson.

Continue eastward on Virginia 3 toward downtown Fredericksburg. The cemetery is adjacent to the highway at the intersection of William and Washington streets.

Chatham   This eighteenth-century Georgian mansion is now the headquarters of the Fredericksburg and Spotsylvania National Military Park. Known during the war as the Lacy House, the imposing structure was a front-line headquarters for a number of Federal generals, including Edwin V. Sumner and Joseph Hooker. A variety of exhibits is open to the public. The front lawn offers a panoramic view of Fredericksburg.

Follow Virginia 3 eastward through Fredericksburg. Immediately after crossing the Rappahannock River, turn left at the first stoplight. Proceed 0.1 mile and turn left into Chatham Lane. It leads to the parking lot for the mansion.

C7   CHANCELLORSVILLE-WILDERNESS   Within a 15-mile radius of Fredericksburg is the greatest concentration of preserved battlefields in Virginia. This area was the scene of intense fighting for more than two years, with at least 600,000 men engaged in combat during that period.

Salem Church   This unobtrusive sanctuary, originally constructed in 1844, was the focal point of bitter fighting on May 3–4, 1863, as Union reinforcements from Fredericksburg sought to come to the aid of Gen. Joseph Hooker and the Army of the Potomac at Chancellorsville. Although the church has undergone extensive restoration, its walls still show the marks of battle. Paintings, exhibits, and artifacts enhance the church grounds.

Salem Church is 1.4 miles west on Virginia 3 from the I-95 intersection.

Zoan Baptist Church   A modern building occupies the site of the wartime wooden structure. The church stands on a swell of ground which was Hooker's farthest advance toward attacking Lee's flank. From there the Federals retreated back to Chancellorsville, thereby leaving themselves susceptible to counterassault.

From Salem Church, continue 2.0 miles west on Virginia 3. Zoan Church is on the left (south) side of the highway.

Chancellorsville   Considered Lee's greatest victory, Chancellorsville is located in a 72-square-mile area of dense woods and thick underbrush known as the Wilderness. Here Federal Gen. Hooker's attempt to turn Lee's left flank inexplicably lost its momentum. Lee, though woefully outnumbered, dispatched Stonewall Jackson on a counterflank march that caught the Union army by surprise. The battle began with skirmishes on May 1, 1863, and lasted the better part of three days. Over 30,000 men were killed, wounded, or captured. The irreplaceable Jackson was among the fatalities.

The National Park Service visitor center at Chancellorsville provides an excellent introduction and tour-start for the battlefield. The best way to see these grounds is by personal automobile tour, using NPS tape recorders as guides. Even the precise route of Jackson's 12-mile flank march can be followed.

The center is 4.0 miles west on Virginia 3 from Zoan Baptist Church (or 7.4 miles from the junction of Virginia 3 and I-95).

Wilderness Battlefield   In 1864 the Army of the Potomac, with General-in-Chief Ulysses S. Grant personally directing its operations, started southward again. Using a strategy similar to Hooker's the previous year, the Federals tried anew to turn Lee's left (western) flank. On May 4 the Union army moved into the darkness of the Wilderness. Lee was waiting. The next two days saw 182,000 men viciously fighting in woods often set afire by bullets. This struggle produced 26,000 casualties and was little more than a momentary check to Grant's advance.

Regrettably, only pieces of the Wilderness battlefield survive today. NPS roads traverse a portion of the area and give access to a handful of roadside markers and monuments. Exhibits are at the Chancellorsville visitor center and on Virginia 20, 1.6 miles from its junction with Virginia 3. An automobile is a must for visiting any part of the battleground.

C8 **SPOTSYLVANIA** From the struggle in the Wilderness, both armies then staged a footrace for control of the vital road junction at Spotsylvania Courthouse. The Southerners barely arrived first and constructed hasty but heavy earthworks. In the next fourteen days (May 8–21, 1864), a number of Federal attacks were made in an effort to break the Confederate lines. The bloodiest engagement of the campaign came in the rain on May 12, when Federals temporarily overran a salient whose northwestern face was known thereafter as the "Bloody Angle."

Recent improvements by the Park Service have made Spotsylvania among the most impressive of Civil War sites. Paved roads run along the works. A walking tour— complete with numbered stops—has been developed for the "Bloody Angle" area. Markers include a plaque showing where a 22-inch oak tree was felled solely by rifle bullets.

To reach Spotsylvania via Grant's advance, proceed west from Chancellorsville on Virginia 3 to the intersection with County 613. Turn left (south) on County 613 and continue 13.7 miles to the Y intersection and exhibit shelter.

If traveling to Spotsylvania from Fredericksburg, take Alternate U.S. 1 south to its junction with Virginia 208. Turn right and continue 6.6 miles to downtown Spotsylvania. At the T intersection in the center of town, turn right on County 613 to reach the battlefield area.

Spotsylvania County Museum   Housed in Old Berea Church, a small brick edifice that suffered heavy damage during the 1864 fighting, this museum contains relics from the battlefields, two dioramas, and other memorabilia. Close to the museum is a Confederate cemetery with the remains of scores of soldiers killed in combat nearby.

The museum is on Virginia 208 at the eastern edge of Spotsylvania.

C9   MASSAPONAX CHURCH   Built in 1859, the rectangular brick structure was a rendezvous point in a number of troop movements, especially in Grant's 1864 Wilderness—to—Cold Harbor campaign. The building is best remembered because of a series of photographs taken of Grant and the ranking generals in the Army of the Potomac, all seated informally in the yard on church pews.

From the intersection of U.S. 1 and Virginia 208 south of Fredericksburg, drive south 3.6 miles on U.S. 1. The church is on the west side of the highway.

C10   GUINEA STATION   It was at this railhead—in the afternoon of May 10, 1863—that Gen. Thomas J. ("Stonewall") Jackson died of pneumonia after being accidentally shot by his own men during the second day's combat at Chancellorsville. Jackson had been brought here following the battle. He was placed in the white clapboard office building of Fairfield, the Chandler plantation. This extremely pious commander died appropriately on the Sabbath after uttering the words: "Let us cross over the river and rest under the shade of the trees."

The house in which Jackson died, plus many furnishings (especially in the death room), are maintained by the National Park Service.

Leave I-95 or U.S. 1 at the Thornburg exit and proceed east on County 606 across the Richmond, Fredericksburg and Potomac Railroad. Bear left alongside the tracks to the shrine parking lot.

C11 **CARMEL CHURCH** A modern edifice occupies the site where the wartime wooden church stood. The area of Carmel Church was the focal point of huge Army of Northern Virginia camps during the winter of 1862–63, and the church's name appears regularly throughout the war in dispatches relative to troop movements north of Richmond.

The crossroads where the church stands is 15 miles south of Thornburg on U.S. 1.

C12 **NORTH ANNA BATTLEFIELD** During May 23– 26, 1864, Grant launched a series of assaults in an effort to break Lee's entrenchments along the south bank of the North Anna River. The attacks failed, and the Army of the Potomac then veered southeastward and continued its advance on Richmond.

None of the battlefield is preserved today. However, 5 miles south of Carmel Church, U.S. 1 crosses the North Anna virtually in the center of the battle area.

CONFEDERATE WORKS ON WILLIS'S HILL, NOW THE SITE OF THE NATIONAL CEMETERY.

HOOKER'S HEADQUARTERS AT CHANCELLORSVILLE, SATURDAY MORNING, MAY 2.

EXPLOSION OF THE MINE.

Southeastern Virginia

To crush secession and restore the Union meant that the Northern forces would have to take the role of invaders and conquer the South. Enormous Federal armies ultimately went into action, as did a naval blockade of the Southern coastline. In the Eastern theater—the area lying between the Appalachian Mountains and the Atlantic Ocean—this strategy caught Virginia in a mighty vise. In addition, Northern leaders earnestly believed that if the Confederate capital could be seized, the Southern nation would collapse. Thus, for four years Richmond was the primary military objective of the North.

Two basic approaches to the capital existed: the overland route by way of Manassas and Fredericksburg and the water route via Hampton-Yorktown and westward up the 80-mile peninsula formed by the York and James rivers. Federal armies tried both approaches, in one instance utilizing the largest amphibious operation that the modern world had ever seen. Losses unprecedented in American history accumulated through the years before Virginia eventually succumbed.

Southeastern Virginia

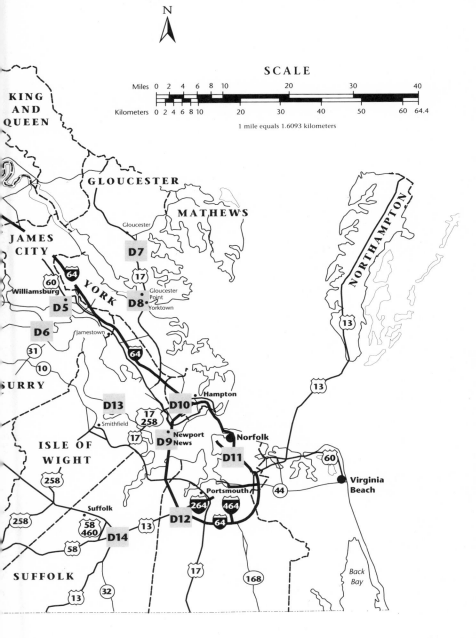

D1 HANOVER COUNTY At this site James E. B. ("Jeb") Stuart received his commission as major general and organized the cavalry corps of Lee's army. On the courthouse lawn is a monument bearing the names of 1,138 county men who fought for the Confederacy. Some 50 names were inadvertently omitted, including Maj. Thomas Doswell and Surgeon Robert Coleman.

The courthouse is in Hanover, 12 miles north of Richmond, at the intersection of U.S. 301 and Virginia 54.

Summer Hill Here, in June 1862, ladies prepared for burial the body of Capt. William Latané, the first Confederate fatality on Stuart's "Ride around McClellan." Latané fell on the road between Hanover and Old Church. At various times during the war, Federal Gens. McClellan, Sheridan, and Grant occupied the home, and it was also used for a time as a military hospital. The modest frame house still belongs to the Newton family, but visitors are welcomed.

One mile south of Hanover on U.S. 301, turn left (east) on County 605 and go 7 miles. A sign points to Summer Hill.

D2 RICHMOND Richmond was literally the heart of the Confederacy. The capital of both the Southern nation and the Confederacy's most important state, Richmond also became the chief manufacturing center in the wartime South, the major rail junction in the Upper South, and hence the sole target for four years of the North's principal army. Major military campaigns in 1862 and 1864–65, a number of Federal raids, and a population quadruple the 38,000 inhabitants of 1860 kept Richmond in turmoil and instability for most of the war. Yet the city stood proud and defiant through all adversity until its abandonment in April 1865.

Today Richmond has more historic attractions than any other city in the South. The visitor who wishes to see all Civil War points of interest should allow a minimum of two days for touring.

Richmond National Battlefield This battlefield park is located on the site of Chimborazo Hospital, where 76,000 patients in the course of the Civil War made it the largest military hospital ever constructed. Exhibits and an audiovisual program at the National Park Service building provide a summary of the years of heavy fighting waged for control of Richmond. A free, easy-to-understand brochure is available for a self-guided 100-mile drive through the major battlefields around the capital. This drive is essential for serious students of the Civil War.

The tour includes Seven Pines, where Confederates checked McClellan's 1862 advance on Richmond in a two-day battle fought largely in mud and swamps. With the wounding at Seven Pines of Gen. Joseph E. Johnston, Robert E. Lee assumed army command and promptly counterattacked. A succession of battles known as the Seven Days campaign followed as Lee sought desperately but in vain to destroy the Federal army and end the war in Virginia.

Today only traces remain of Mechanicsville, Gaines's Mill, Savage Station, White Oak Swamp, Frayser's Farm, and Malvern Hill. Yet in these engagements the Confederates reversed pending defeat and, at a staggering cost of 25 percent losses, repulsed the second major Union effort to seize Richmond.

Also on this tour is the partially restored battlefield of

Cold Harbor. Here, on June 3, 1864, Gen. U. S. Grant rashly ordered dawn frontal assaults against Lee's heavily fortified lines. What ensued has been termed the worst slaughter of Americans in the nation's history. Some 7,200 Federals were shot down in 20 minutes. Thereafter, Grant resumed his flanking movements, crossed the James, and invested Petersburg. A number of forts involved in the 1864–65 besiegement are part of the auto tour.

The National Park Service headquarters building in Richmond is at 3215 E. Broad Street (the city's main thoroughfare).

Museum of the Confederacy This two-building complex consists of a new exhibit hall and the three-story home that served as the White House of the Southern nation. The largest extant collection of Confederate artifacts is here, including the field uniforms of Gens. Lee, Jackson, Stuart, and Joseph E. Johnston. The 1818 Brockenbrough mansion, which served as the official residence of President Jefferson Davis, has been extensively renovated to appear as it did during the war years. Admission charge.

The White House and its adjacent museum are at the corner of East Clay and 12th streets, 2 blocks north of Broad Street.

Valentine Museum Built in 1812 and donated to the City of Richmond 70 years later, this is a depository principally of costumes and other fine arts material. The chief Civil War attraction is a plaster cast of Edward V. Valentine's most famous sculpture, the recumbent figure of Gen. Robert E. Lee. Admission charge.

The home and its adjoining historic structures stand

at the southwest corner of Clay and 11th streets, a block west of the Museum of the Confederacy.

State Capitol Designed by Thomas Jefferson, this building was the seat of the Confederate government. It was inside the marble edifice, in April 1861, that Robert E. Lee assumed command of all Virginia forces. In February 1862 Jefferson Davis delivered his inaugural address at the base of the Washington Statue in the northwest corner of the Capitol grounds, and the statue became the major symbol on the Confederate Seal. Also on the grounds of the Capitol are bronze likenesses of Confederate notables Gen. Stonewall Jackson, Gov. William Smith, and Surgeon Hunter McGuire. Guided tours of the Capitol itself are conducted on a regular basis.

Capitol Square is situated one block south of Broad Street between 9th and 12th streets.

Saint Paul's Episcopal Church This stately sanctuary, dedicated in 1845, is widely known as the "Church of the Confederacy." Jefferson Davis received confirmation here early in the war, and on April 2, 1865, he was attending morning prayer services when he received word from Lee that the Richmond-Petersburg defenses had been broken. The Lee Memorial Window and pew plaques are some of the church's leading Civil War features.

Across the street from Capitol Square, Saint Paul's is on the southwest corner of Grace and 9th streets.

Monument Avenue This wide boulevard is so named because of five large statues interspersed along its route. The monuments are of J. E. B. Stuart, Robert E. Lee, Jefferson Davis, Thomas J. Jackson, and Matthew Fontaine Maury.

The avenue is basically a continuation of Franklin Street, with its eastern end at Lombardy Street. It is parallel to, and 2 blocks south of, Broad Street.

Battle Abbey Now the headquarters of the Virginia Historical Society, this majestic building was completed as a Confederate memorial hall in 1913. On display are Southern battleflags, portraiture, and weapons. One room houses a gigantic mural series by French artist Charles Hoffbauer of battle scenes in Virginia. Within the building is probably the best research library on the Civil War in the Old Dominion.

This museum—reference library is at 428 N. Boulevard, 4 blocks south of Broad Street.

Hollywood Cemetery Second in renown only to Arlington National Cemetery, this 115-acre tract opened in 1849 and derived its name from large holly trees located on the grounds. Here will be found the largest number of distinguished Virginians buried in one place. Hollywood also contains the graves of 15,000 Confederate soldiers who perished during the war. A map-guide to the more prominent graves (including those of three presidents) is available at the cemetery office just inside the gate. The driveways are quite narrow, and funeral services may occasionally impede travel in some sections.

The entrance to Hollywood Cemetery is at Cherry and Albemarle streets. From Broad street, proceed south on Belvidere (U.S. 1−60−301) for 7 blocks. Then turn right (west) on Albemarle Street for 3 blocks.

Belle Isle On this island in the James River stood one of the war's chief prison camps. Some 6,000 Federals were confined here at the prison's peak. The island is not open to the public, but some preliminary planning has been done to make the island into a civic and historic park.

As one continues southward on Belvidere and crosses the river, Belle Isle is visible just below the bridge on the right-hand (west) side.

Yellow Tavern On May 11, 1864, near a way station along the Brock Turnpike, occurred a sharp cavalry fight between the horsemen of Gens. Philip Sheridan and Jeb Stuart. The 31-year-old Confederate commander was shot near the end of the action and died the following day from loss of blood. The spot where the "Gray Cavalier" was mortally wounded is marked and maintained by the United Daughters of the Confederacy.

From I-95 North, drive west 0.4 mile on Parham Road to the intersection with U.S. 1. Turn north for 2.1 miles. Turn right (east) on Francis Road and go 0.5 mile to Telegraph Road, then bear right on Telegraph Road for 0.1 mile. The Stuart Memorial is on the right-hand side of the road.

D3   DREWRY'S BLUFF Although included in the automobile tour of the Richmond-area battlefields, the beauty and the comparative isolation of this site make it deserving of special mention. The bluff is on a bend in the James River, 7 miles south of Richmond. Early in 1862, Confederates erected strong fortifications here to guard the water approach to the capital. On May 15 of that year, Southern cannoneers at Drewry's Bluff (or Fort Darling, as it is sometimes called) repulsed an attack by a Federal fleet that included the celebrated ironclad *Monitor*. The Confederate naval academy was established here the following year, and Drewry's Bluff was the scene of more fighting in May 1864.

A walking tour of the elaborate remains of the fort has been developed by the National Park Service. A painting and huge Columbiad cannon are on display at the installation's most scenic spot.

From downtown Richmond, go 7.4 miles south on I-95 to Exit 7 (Chippenham Parkway). Turn right to U.S. 1, then left (south) on U.S. 1 for 2.4 miles. At the spotlight, bear left on County 656—Bellwood Road. Immediately beyond an overpass, turn left on Fort Darling Road and follow signs to the parking area.

D4 CHARLES CITY COUNTY No major action took place in this county, but Federal armies passed through the district—and left their marks upon it—in both 1862 and 1864.

Salem Church One of the oldest Methodist churches in America, Salem became an 1864 field hospital for wounded and sick soldiers on both sides. The building no longer stands, but a cemetery adjacent to the site contains the remains of a number of Confederates—including a member of the "C. S. Detective Corps."

Starting at the courthouse in Charles City, drive west on Virginia 5 for 5.6 miles. Turn north on County 609 for 3.5 miles. The cemetery and site of Salem Church are on the left.

Berkeley Plantation This was the birthplace of President William Henry Harrison. General George B. McClellan used the home for a headquarters during the 1862 Peninsular campaign. When Federal Gen. Daniel Butterfield occupied the mansion that same year, he conceived the bugle call that became "Taps." The plantation served also as a hospital and signal station. On most wartime maps, Berkeley is called Harrison's Landing. Admission charge.

The entrance to the plantation is 6.6 miles west of Charles City on Virginia 5.

Shirley Plantation   An estate whose beginnings date from the early 1600s, Shirley Plantation has a history that spans 300 years. The mother of Robert E. Lee was born here, and the future Confederate general enjoyed many visits to Shirley. The home was a Federal hospital during McClellan's 1862 advance on Richmond. When Federal troops ransacked the home later that summer, Lee reputedly became angrier than at any other time in the Civil War. The mansion is still owned by the Carter family. Admission charge.

From Charles City, it is 9.9 miles west on Virginia 5 to the plantation entrance.

D5   WILLIAMSBURG   This first capital of Virginia became a key point in the Confederate defenses of the peninsula. Here, on May 5, 1862, the initial battle of the Peninsular campaign took place. The major fighting raged east of the town, although skirmishes occurred in the streets and on the campus of the College of William and Mary. The Wren Building, the main building on the campus, was burned by Federals; in 1895 the federal government made partial restitution.

Archer's Hope   At this inlet of the James River, Confederates threw up gun emplacements to challenge any Federal ships advancing up the river. Vestiges of these works are evident today.

From Williamsburg, proceed 5.1 miles south on the Colonial Parkway.

D6 JAMESTOWN Here, where America began, will be found two extensive remains of Southern earthworks. Legend has it that the trenches were constructed in 1861 by slaves from Surry County plantations across the river.

The Civil War reminders are prominently situated along the waterfront.

D7 GLOUCESTER COUNTY This county was the scene of several minor skirmishes during the war. A monument on the courthouse lawn at Gloucester contains the names of all county men who lost their lives in the conflict.

Gloucester Tourist Information Center Among the information available here is a list of all graves of known Confederate soldiers, as well as directions to the various cemeteries in the area.

The center occupies the old Debtors Prison on the west side of U.S. 17 Business in downtown Gloucester.

Ware Church Women of the community kept this Espicopal church open and functioning regularly throughout the war. It remained free from harm in spite of Federal occupation and occasional skirmishes.

From the center of Gloucester, proceed 0.2 mile on Virginia 14. The church is on the south side of the highway.

Abingdon Church Not as fortunate as Ware Church, this house of worship suffered the indignity of being used as a stable. However, the federal government later reimbursed the congregation for damages done.

The building is on U.S. 17, 1.5 miles south of Gloucester and just beyond the junction with County 614.

Gloucester Point Extensive earthworks were here for the duration of the Civil War. Some remnants are visible opposite Tindall's Point Bridge.

Continue south from Gloucester on U.S. 17 to the bridge spanning the York River. Gloucester Point stands at the north end of the bridge.

D8 YORKTOWN Early in the war, Confederates began fortifying the Virginia peninsula against a possible Federal thrust on Richmond. Three defense lines were built from the James to the York rivers. Time has erased all traces of the first and third positions. Yet much of the second, strongest line of works, extending from Fort Crafford on Mulberry Island to Yorktown, remains in evidence. The Confederate defenses included man-made lakes as well as entrenchments.

It was at Yorktown, in March-April 1862, that Federal Gen. George M. McClellan landed his massive Army of the Potomac for an advance on Richmond up the peninsula. This amphibious operation involved the transfer from Washington to Yorktown of 121,500 men, 59 batteries of artillery, 15,000 animals, 1,100 supply wagons plus tons of military goods too numerous to itemize.

Colonial National Historical Park Here Gen. John B. Magruder, commanding Southern forces on the peninsula in 1861, reinforced many of the Revolutionary War trenches utilized by the British. It is now difficult to ascertain precisely which earthworks in the Yorktown park figured as well in the Civil War, but this National Park Service site offers a stunning view of earthen defenses.

From U.S. 17, just east of the town of Yorktown, proceed on the Colonial Parkway 0.7 mile to the park headquarters. Trenches employed in the Civil War will be on the right as you enter the parking lot.

Yorktown National Cemetery Established in 1866, this cemetery contains 2,200 graves, mostly of Union dead. A small Confederate graveyard is located nearby.

The national cemetery is on County 704 inside the Yorktown battlefield park.

WHARF, YORK RIVER.   MCCLELLAN'S HEADQUARTERS.   NELSON HOUSE.

VIEW OF MAIN STREET, YORKTOWN—THE UNION TROOPS MARCHING IN.
From a sketch made May 4 186?

Jones Mill Pond Earthworks   Here will be found another example of the elaborate trench network erected by the
Confederates in their defense of the peninsula.
   From the Yorktown Visitor Center at the park, go 9.2
miles on the Colonial Parkway.

D9   NEWPORT NEWS   Today's teeming metropolis is a far
cry from the village that existed at the time of the Civil
War. Yet in spite of its size then, Newport News figured
prominently in the 1861–62 Virginia campaigns.

Newport News Park   The largest municipal park east of the
Mississippi River, this recreation area also contains superb reminders of the Civil War. Confederate Gen. Magruder made extensive use of existing dams in preparing
his defense lines. He also erected other levees so as to be
able to flood the lowlands in case of a Federal advance.
Inside the park is Dam No. 1, the scene of a sharp fight
on April 16, 1862, when Vermont troops attempted un-
successfully to break the Confederate position. This unusual battlefield remains basically as it was. An interpretive center and walking tours are accessible to the
public.
   More avid and athletic history buffs can take a 3-mile
hike in the park to Wynn's Mill, where stand in virginal
state the most impressive earthworks in Virginia.
   Exit from I-64 onto Virginia 105 East. Drive 0.1 mile
to the intersection with Virginia 143. Turn left (west)
and continue for 0.3 mile to the park entrance. The interpretive center is 0.9 mile inside the park on the right,
with the battlefield extending on both sides of the road.

Fort Eustis   Two Civil War attractions exist inside this army
base. One is the U.S. Army Transportation Museum. Al-

though slanted heavily toward recent military history, this elaborate display includes several Civil War exhibits. Also on the fort grounds is Fort Crafford, a star-shaped bastion on Mulberry Island which anchored the right flank of the Confederacy's main defense line across the peninsula. The earthworks and gun emplacements of Fort Crafford are remarkably well preserved. However, the site is in an isolated area of Fort Eustis. Persons wishing to visit the riverside area should check first with Transportation Museum officials to determine when Fort Crafford is open for inspection.

To reach Fort Eustis, take Virginia 105 west from I-64 for 1.4 miles. Follow museum signs inside the installation.

The Mariners Museum   Artillery pieces and exhibits on Civil War naval affairs form a small part of this extraordinary museum. Allow a half-day to make a thorough visit. Admission charge.

From I-64, take U.S. 17 (Exit 9) south for 1.5 miles. Continue south on Virginia 312 for 3.1 miles to the museum entrance.

War Memorial Museum of Virginia   This large depository has 20,000 indoor and outdoor exhibits relative to Virginia soldiers from pre-Revolutionary times to the present. Uniforms, accoutrements, and artwork of the 1860s are displayed. Admission charge.

Leave I-64 at the junction with U.S. 258 and proceed south for 3.4 miles. Turn west on U.S. 60 for 0.4 mile. The museum is on the south side of the highway.

Monitor-Merrimack Overlook   This magnificent view of Hampton Roads is situated near the site of Camp Butler, an early Federal installation that was used in the last months of the war as an internment camp for Southern prisoners of war. Here, on March 9, 1862, scores of persons gathered to watch the duel between the U.S.S. *Monitor* and the C.S.S. *Virginia* (formerly the U.S.S. *Merrimack*). Weather permitting, Forts Monroe and Wool, the Norfolk naval yard, and other points are clearly visible from this overlook.

At Exit 6 on I-64, proceed south toward Newport News on Virginia 167 for 4.6 miles to the second roadside historical marker. The first marker, "First Battle of Ironclads," is misplaced and should be located two miles farther west.

D10 HAMPTON On June 10, 1861, just outside Hampton, occurred the battle of Big Bethel. It was the first significant engagement of the war in Virginia. Two months later, Confederates raided Hampton to prevent its occupation by Federals; and in the ensuing action, the town was virtually demolished.

Syms-Eaton Museum This small depository contains uniforms and interpretive exhibits on Hampton during the war period. The Hampton Information Center is directly across the highway.

From I-64, go east toward Fort Monroe on U.S. 258 (Mercury Boulevard) for 1.5 miles.

Big Bethel Some 4,000 green Federals attacked 1,500 equally untested Confederates. Two hours of confused fighting followed before the Northerners fled from the field. Unfortunately, the site of the battle is now beneath the Big Bethel Reservoir and inside Langley Air Force Base. Two monuments and a small cemetery are the only mementos.

Take U.S. 258 south from I-64 to the first stoplight. Turn right (west) on Todds Lane for 1.6 miles to the intersection with Big Bethel Road. After bearing right on Big Bethel Road, continue 3.3 miles to the markers.

Fort Monroe Any visit to the lower peninsula should include a lengthy stop at this base, traditionally known as "The Gibraltar of Chesapeake Bay." Construction of the casemated and moat-encircled fort began in 1819 and consumed fifteen years. Robert E. Lee was a principal engineer. During the Civil War, the fort was headquarters for Federal Gens. Benjamin F. Butler and George B. McClellan. Lincoln and Grant both were guests there, and Confederate President Jefferson Davis was imprisoned in one of the casemates following his May 1865 capture.

Of interest today are the Jefferson Davis Casemate Museum (the logical and necessary starting point), Robert E. Lee's quarters, the Chapel of the Centurion, the Lincoln Gun, and the view of the harbor entrance.

From I-64, take either Virginia 143 or 169 and follow signs to Fort Monroe. Military police at the fort's gate will provide directions to the Casemate Museum inside the old bastion.

Fort Wool Situated on a man-made island in the middle of the Hampton Roads channel, this abandoned army base is often called "Rip Raps" after the shoal on which it rests. The original installation was known as Fort Calhoun and was completed in 1858 after twenty-eight years of labor. Designed to strengthen the defenses of the harbor's entrance, Fort Wool was a focal point in the 1862 Federal bombardment of Norfolk. President Lincoln watched the artillery barrage from its ramparts.

The island is now owned by the City of Hampton and

clearly visible from any vantage point. At the present time, however, it is not open to the public.

D11 NORFOLK Ten percent of Norfolk's 14,000 residents perished in an 1855 epidemic of yellow fever. The town—Virginia's principal port—had barely recovered from this tragedy when civil war exploded in its midst. In April 1861 Federals burned and abandoned the navy yard. Union forces reoccupied Norfolk in May 1862 and exercised strong and sometimes brutal control over the city for the remainder of the war.

Confederate Monument Located at the intersection of Main Street and Commerce Place, this 1907 memorial pays tribute to the men of Norfolk who served in Confederate forces.

Old Town Hall Here, in an elaborate ceremony, Federal troops triumphantly raised "Old Glory" when the city was captured in 1862. The building is now the MacArthur Memorial and is located on MacArthur Square in the downtown area.

D12 PORTSMOUTH The Portsmouth Naval Shipyard has been an active producer of warships for over a century. Amid its bustling activity today are several reminders of achievements of yesteryear.

Portsmouth Naval Shipyard Museum Numerous relics and displays here include items pertaining to the South's first ironclad warship, the C.S.S. *Virginia.*

The museum is at 2 High Street, alongside the Elizabeth River.

U.S. Naval Hospital A stone cairn memorializes some 300 men lost in the destruction of the U.S.S. *Cumberland* and *Congress* in a March 8, 1862, attack by the C.S.S. *Virginia*. On adjacent grounds to the hospital are the graves of many Confederate and Federal soldiers.

The hospital stands at the north end of Green Street.

D13   FORT BOYKIN Dating back to 1623, this is one of the oldest fortifications in America. The earthen work was improved during the War of 1812 to its present seven-pointed-star design. In 1862 fire from Federal gunboats forced the Southern garrison to abandon the installation. Confederate soldier-poet Sidney Lanier wrote at least two poems while stationed here in the war's first months. The 15-acre tract is now being renovated and will shortly become a state park.

Fort Boykin is 4 miles north of Smithfield. Take Business Route 10 from downtown to the junction with unpaved County 673. Proceed on County 673 to the intersection with County 705. The fort stands at that point alongside the James River.

D14   SUFFOLK At least eight skirmishes were fought in and around Suffolk. Yet the town's most conspicuous period came April 11–May 4, 1863, when Confederates under Gen. James Longstreet laid seige to Suffolk under the assumption that Gen. John Peck's 25,000 Federals inside the town were about to embark on a northern drive toward Richmond. The movement never materialized, and the siege proved ineffective.

Kilby's Law Office This building served as a repository for valuable papers, books, and church records during the war years. The front part of the structure retains its nineteenth-century appearance.

Located at 347 N. Main Street, the building is now the Suffolk Senior Citizens Center.

Riddick's Folly   General Peck's headquarters during the Suffolk campaign was in this home. The dwelling dates back to 1839 and is soon to undergo restoration.

The home is at 510 N. Main Street. It is open by appointment without charge.

Old Nansemond County Court House   The Union army used this structure as a barracks and headquarters for much of the war. It now houses local courts.

Easily recognizable, the courthouse stands at 524 N. Main Street.

Godwin House   Constructed in 1830 but recently altered by minor improvements, the dwelling was used as a hospital by Federal forces during the siege of the city. It is not open to the public buy may be seen from the roadway.

The home is at 504 W. Washington Street.

Cedar Hill Cemetery   In use many years before the outbreak of civil war, this burial ground contains scores of graves from the conflict of the 1860s. A Confederate monument is one of the dominant markers in the cemetery.

It is located at Main Street and Constance Road.

D15   PETERSBURG   Next to Richmond, Petersburg was the scene of more Civil War action than any other community in Virginia. The nine-month siege of the city in 1864–65 remains the longest such operation on American soil. Some 35 miles of parallel earthworks extended in unbroken lines from east of Richmond to southwest of Petersburg. Constant pounding by Federals of Lee's thin but defiant ranks during the siege produced over

65,000 Northern and Southern casualties. Throughout the long campaign, Confederate Gen. John B. Gordon noted, "Lee's Miserables" were occupied in "fighting famine from within and Grant from without." The dozens of engagements fought around Petersburg make the area the largest battlefield in America.

Historic Petersburg Information Center   This starting point for any tour of the city is located on Washington Street, just to the west of I-95 at Exit 3. The center offers personal assistance as well as printed material on the Petersburg area.

Petersburg National Battlefield   A variety of attractions makes this one of the National Park Service's most popular sites. The visitor center has a 17-minute lighted map presentation of the Petersburg campaign. Behind the center are a display of cannon barrels, an original artillery fort, and a seacoast mortar of the "Dictator" type. An automobile tour with numbered stops winds past forts and rebuilt works and culminates at the Crater, scene of one of the war's most unique and costly battles. For those who wish to examine a larger and more undeveloped segment of the siege lines, a self-guided, 16-mile auto tour passes along sites on both public and private property. Detailed leaflets on all of these points of interest are obtainable at the Park headquarters.

From I-95's Exit 3, proceed east on Virginia 36 for 2.4 miles to the battlefield park entrance.

U.S. Army Quartermaster's Museum   This large and elaborate display contains weapons, emblems, and equipment spanning all of America's wars.

The museum is inside Fort Lee, which is adjacent to

the battlefield park. Signs along Virginia 36 East provide easy directions.

Blandford Cemetery   The massed graves of 30,000 Confederates are in this huge cemetery, which was established over 270 years ago. Local tradition insists that Memorial Day had its origin here on June 9, 1866. No visit to Petersburg is complete without a tour of Blandford Church. The two-century-old building, located just inside the main gate of the cemetery, is a memorial to Confederate dead. Fifteen Charles Tiffany stained-glass windows radiate a beauty—especially in late afternoon—that cannot be described. A nearby museum offers a slide program and exhibits pertaining to the church's history.

Again utilizing Exit 3 off I-95, follow U.S. 301 south for 0.2 mile. The cemetery is on the left.

Siege Museum   One of the state's newest and more formal displays, this museum highlights the events and hardships of the long Federal envelopment of the city. Movie star and Petersburg native Joseph Cotten narrates a film which dramatically retells the city's wartime story.

Located at 15 W. Bank Street, the Siege Museum is in a renovated area of the downtown. Take Exit 4 west from I-95.

Saint Paul's Episcopal Church   A marker denotes the pew where Gen. Lee worshiped during the nine-month campaign for Petersburg. Two other Confederate generals, William H. F. ("Rooney") Lee (the commanding general's son) and George E. Pickett, were married in this church. A stained-glass window to the memory of Lee, a nave that remains as it looked at the time of the war, and "the only notable antebellum set of church bells in Virginia" are other features of Saint Paul's.

Leave I-95 at Exit 3. Proceed west for 5 blocks, then turn right to 110 N. Union Street.

Turnbull House This reconstructed home served as Lee's headquarters from November 1864 until the Federal breakthrough in April 1865. It is privately owned.

The house stands on the north side of U.S. 1, approximately 1 mile south of the Appomattox River.

D16 DINWIDDIE COUNTY More than 45 engagements took place within this county in the last ten months of the conflict. Dinwiddie County is estimated to have over 50 miles of extant fortifications as well as remnants of 50 forts and batteries. Directions to the more accessible of these sites may be obtained at the Petersburg National Battlefield headquarters.

Poplar Grove National Cemetery Situated on ground where severe fighting occurred in 1864 for control of the nearby railroad, this cemetery contains the graves of more than 6,000 soldiers—4,000 unknown.

It is located on County 675, a half-mile south of the Petersburg city limits and just east of I-85.

Five Forks At this obscure point, on the afternoon of April 1, 1865, Gen. Philip H. Sheridan launched massive Federal assaults that broke the Southern lines after a nine-month stalemate. Lee's outnumbered army, starving on its feet, then started on a 100-mile "corridor of sorrows" that would end at Appomattox.

A roadside marker about Five Forks is on U.S. 460, 5 miles west of Sutherland. The actual battlefield, none of which is preserved, can be reached by proceeding west from Sutherland on U.S. 460 for 6 miles, then south on County 627 for 4 miles to its junction with County 613.

Burnt Quarter   Sheridan's headquarters during the battle was in this plantation home of the Gilliam family. The home was also the scene of at least one session of Gen. G. K. Warren's subsequent court of inquiry. Burnt Quarter is well maintained and contains many of the furnishings of the Civil War period.

It is situated on County 613, 1 mile west of the Five Forks junction.

D17 **"BEEFSTEAK RAID"**   In September 1864 Confederate cavalry under Gen. Wade Hampton galloped behind Federal lines and captured an entire herd of cattle for Lee's starving army. The cattle were driven southwestward down a long stretch of County 626, east of the junction with Virginia 35. The Donnan House, now in private possession and just to the east of this intersection, stood at the time. Confederate troopers asked directions here; and in return for the information, they gave the destitute family a cow too disabled to be driven farther.

D18 **STONY CREEK**   This small community was the scene of several engagements in the last year of the war. In one such action (June 28, 1864), Federals retreated so hastily that they discarded furniture, silverware, livestock, personal effects, and 1,000 blacks—all of which they had confiscated elsewhere. This pillaging later produced a Federal investigation.

West of Stony Creek, and south of the intersection of Virginia 40 and County 681, is Sappony Church, the site of a June 1864 skirmish. Today a circular patch in the pediment marks where a shell struck the building. A Bible grazed by a rifle ball can also be seen here.

D19 JARRATT Only a village in 1861–65, this railroad stop was burned in May 1864 by Federal cavalry. Seven months later, the tracks in and around here were wrecked beyond repair. The only dwelling in Jarratt not destroyed was the Humphrey Grigg Tavern. It was spared from the torch reputedly because Federals used it as a headquarters.

The tavern, now privately owned, is at Old Halifax Road and County 631 in Jarratt.

D20 COURTLAND In antebellum days, Courtland was called Jerusalem. Near here, on the night of August 21, 1831, a demented slave named Nat Turner led a band of blacks on a murdering spree that claimed the lives of 57 whites, mostly women and children. Hastily organized posses brutally suppressed the uprising, and Turner and a dozen of his followers were tried, convicted, and hanged. The Nat Turner Insurrection was the bloodiest overture to civil war in Virginia.

The scene of the insurrection were the properties bordering Virginia 35 for approximately three miles north of Courtland.

Baptist Church This structure, in the center of Courtland, was one of the town's most prominent buildings during the war. It was pressed into service as a hospital in 1863 when an epidemic of measles swept through the nearby army camps. Several soldiers (mostly members of Hood's Texas Brigade) succumbed to the disease and are buried in the cemetery behind the church.

THE BATTLE OF SAVAGE'S STATION.
From a sketch made at the time.

"WITH FATE AGAINST THEM."
From the painting by Gilbert Gaul.

South Central Virginia

This section of the Piedmont was the center of the Upper South's money crop: tobacco, which, to Johnny Rebs and Billy Yanks alike, was either a luxury or a bartering item worth its weight in gold. Southside Virginia did not feel the hard hand of an invading army until the last week of hostilities. Still, the conflict altered appreciably and permanently the lives of the small farmers and merchants who comprised the bulk of the region's society. These Virginians had been among the most ardent of secessionists, and there was irony in the fact that the Civil War ended in their midst.

South Central Virginia

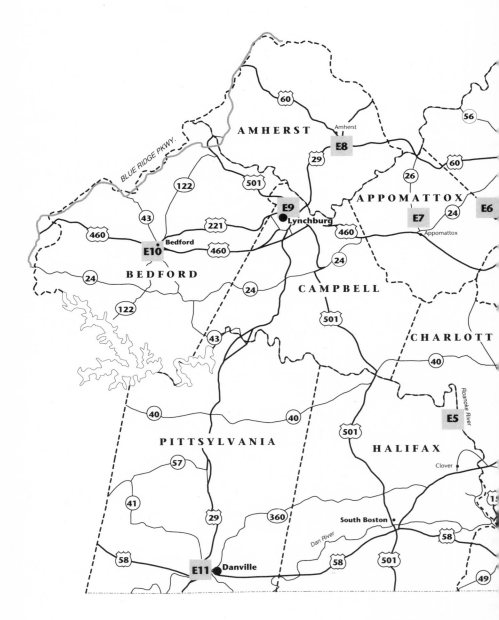

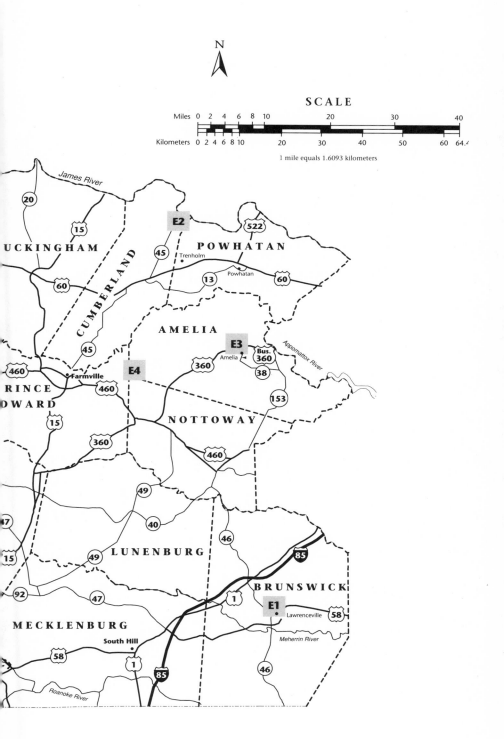

E1 LAWRENCEVILLE The county courthouse, a red brick structure with tall Ionic portico, was the scene of a personal drama during the war. Union troops were approaching the town and its fall was imminent. The county clerk, realizing the impossibility of hiding the huge volumes that contained the county's records, spread his Masonic apron on his desk and left his office door open. Federals briefly occupied the town, then departed. The clerk returned to his office to find that the records had not been touched.

The courthouse is on U.S. 58 Business in downtown Lawrenceville.

E2 DERWENT To this modest two-story frame house, in July 1865, Lee and his family moved to escape the crowded atmosphere of postwar Richmond. Lee lived here for three months before departing for Lexington to assume the presidency of Washington College.

On U.S. 60 proceed 8 miles west of Powhatan, turn right (north) on County 629 to Trenholm, then follow signs.

E3 AMELIA On April 4, 1865, Lee's retreating and impoverished army reached here in hopes of securing food from cars of the Richmond and Danville Railroad. No supplies materialized, forcing the Southern army to resume its westward march the following day. The Jackson Library in Amelia contains some items of interest, and in the clerk's office at the county courthouse is an unofficial roster of all Amelia County soldiers.

Confederate Monument One of the more impressive memorials to Virginia Confederate soldiers, this monument stands on the courthouse lawn.

E4 SAYLER'S CREEK BATTLEFIELD HISTORICAL STATE PARK Here took place the final major battle of the war in Virginia. On April 6, 1865, Federals encircled the rear third of Lee's retreating forces. Fighting lasted through the afternoon and resulted in more than 7,000 Southerners captured, including eight generals and a large number of high-ranking officers. As broken fragments of Confederate columns stumbled to catch up with what was left of the main body, Lee looked at the scene and exclaimed: "My God! Has the army dissolved?" Today some 220 acres of the battlefield have been developed into a state park.

From U.S. 360, 9 miles west of Amelia, or from U.S. 460, 8 miles east of Farmville, turn north on County 617 for 1.7 miles to the park boundary.

E5 STAUNTON RIVER BRIDGE In June 1864 two Federal cavalry regiments attempted to sever the Richmond and Danville Railroad by destroying the high bridge over the Staunton River. An undersized Confederate regiment, assisted by 600 local citizens, repulsed the Federals after sharp fighting. A modern metal trestle now stands at the site, but remnants of earthworks exist along the river's edge. On the lawn of the Legion Hall in downtown South Boston is the barrel of one of the Confederate cannon used in the engagement.

From U.S. 360 at Clover, go north on Virginia 92. Turn left on County 600, cross the R&D (now Southern) tracks, and drive for approximately 4 miles. Turn right on County 855, recross the railroad, and continue on this dirt road for 0.3 mile to the battle site.

E6 BUCKINGHAM COUNTY County 636, which traverses Buckingham County, is the main route which

Lee's army followed on its way to a rendezvous with history at Appomattox. From Farmville, take Virginia 45 north for 5 miles, then left on County 636 at Raines Tavern. At a point 3.5 miles west on 636 is Clifton, the home where Gen. U. S. Grant spent the night of April 8, 1865, and where he corresponded with Lee about a possible surrender of the Confederate army. The home is not open to the public.

E7 APPOMATTOX At this quiet village, far from the arenas of bloodshed, four years of war in Virginia came to a close. Lee's ragged army retreated to this point on April 8, 1865, only to find itself surrounded by the Federal Army of the Potomac. In the afternoon of the following day—Palm Sunday—Lee met personally with his Union counterpart. The terms of surrender offered by Grant and accepted by Lee were the most lenient for any civil war in history, with the result that the legacy of bitterness so associated with civil wars did not occur in this nation. The Civil War ended here, but it would be more appropriate to say that modern America began here.

The National Park Service has restored a dozen buildings in this community. Several exhibits as well as convenient walking tours are available. From U.S. 460 in present-day Appomattox, take Virginia 24 for 3 miles northeast to the park entrance.

E8 AMHERST A county historical museum in Amherst has a display treating of the Civil War period. The museum is on Taylor Street, one block from Main Street and near the county courthouse.

Fourteen miles east of Amherst on U.S. 60 at the crossing of the James River stand the abutments of a covered bridge burned in 1865 by Sheridan's cavalry.

THE CAPTURE OF EWELL'S CORPS, APRIL 6, 1865.

E9 LYNCHBURG The junction of three rail lines and a major east-west canal made Lynchburg an important supply depot during the war. The town also contained two camps of instruction and several military hospitals, in addition to being a rendezvous center for Confederate troops. Lynchburg was the site of a brief military campaign in June 1864.

Fort Early Named for Gen. Jubal A. Early, who commanded the Southern defenses and who made Lynchburg his home from 1869 until his death in 1894, this partially restored redoubt is the only earthen reminder of the battle of Lynchburg. A simple monument to Early stands nearby.

Remnants of Fort Early are located on Fort Avenue

(U.S. 29 Business) and Vermont Avenue. The grounds are easily viewed but not open to the public.

Spring Hill Cemetery Here will be found the graves of Confederate Gens. Early and James Dearing, cavalry commander Thomas T. Munford, Sen. John Warwick Daniel, and a child of Gen. Jeb Stuart.

The cemetery, also on Fort Avenue, is between Lancaster Street and Wythe Road.

Confederate Monument Designed by James O. Scott of Lynchburg and erected in 1898, this statue of a Southern infantryman honors all sons of the area who served as soldiers in the war.

This marker is at the top of Monument Terrace and across the street from the Old City Court House, which is currently being developed into a museum of Lynchburg's history.

Daniel Monument John Warwick Daniel served on Early's staff, received a serious wound at the battle of the Wilderness, but later enjoyed a distinguished career as orator and U.S. senator. This unique memorial to "The Lame Lion of Lynchburg" was the creation of Sir Moses Ezekiel, one of the most famous of the postwar sculptors.

The Daniel monument stands at the intersection of Park Avenue, 9th Street, and Floyd Street.

Jackson Funeral Boat In Riverside Park, at 2240 Rivermont Avenue, is a fragment of the hull of the canalboat *Marshall*. This vessel transported the body of Gen. Stonewall Jackson from Lynchburg to its final destination in Lexington. The park is on a picturesque bluff overlooking the James River.

E10   BEDFORD   A sparsely settled area at the time of the war, Bedford County nevertheless contributed over 600 artillerists and infantrymen to the Confederate cause. The town of Bedford (then known as Liberty) was heavily damaged by Federal troops during the June 1864 Lynchburg campaign.

Confederate Memorial   This stone shaft, dedicated in 1909, honors all county men who saw service in the conflict.

The monument is on the west lawn of the Bedford County Courthouse, on Main Street in downtown Bedford.

Bedford City/County Museum   In this relatively small depository are a number of artifacts from the Civil War period. Restricted visiting hours are in effect. Admission charge.

Located one block east of the courthouse, the museum is at 205 E. Main Street.

Piedmont Hospital   Originally a boy's school that began operation in 1849, this building served as a military hospital for most of the war. It is now the Liberty Manor Home for the Elderly, but it retains its wartime appearance. Visitors may inspect the first floor of the premises.

The structure is at 812 E. Main Street.

Longwood Cemetery   Five Confederate hospitals were established in and around Bedford. Years after the war, the remains of soldiers who had died of sickness and wounds were placed in a single grave in this cemetery. Today a tall obelisk stands over the final resting place of 192 Southern soldiers and a Confederate nurse.

From Main Street in downtown Bedford, go north on Bridge Street for 0.3 mile. The cemetery is on the right.

E11 DANVILLE This city was the western terminus during wartime for the vital Richmond and Danville Railroad. Situated at the falls of the Dan River, it too became an important supply base for Confederate military efforts in Virginia. In the last days of the war, six of Danville's tobacco warehouses served as prisons for captured Federal soldiers. Lack of necessities, plus a smallpox epidemic, caused the deaths of some 1,400 of the prisoners. When Lee's thin lines at Richmond and Petersburg broke under attacks on April 1–2, 1865, the Confederate government shifted to Danville; and for a week the city was the capital of the Southern nation.

Prisons Two of the six warehouse-prisons still stand. They are at 300 Lynn Street and 514 High Street in the downtown area. Visitors will need local assistance in finding them.

Danville Museum of Fine Arts and History This antebellum home of Maj. William T. Sutherlin, a Confederate quartermaster, is often called "the last Capitol of the Confederacy." Jefferson Davis lived here during April 3–10, 1865, and it was from here that he issued his last presidential proclamation.

The mansion is at 975 Main Street, west of the business district.

National Cemetery Here will be found the graves of 1,100 Federals who died while prisoners of war. The cemetery is at 721 Lee Street, alongside the tracks of the Southern Railway. From the Sutherlin Mansion, proceed south on Holbrook Avenue 6 blocks to the stop sign. Turn left onto Stokes Street and go one long block to the dead end. Turn right for one block, then left on Lee street.

Southwestern Virginia

Mountains isolate the southwestern tip of the Old Dominion from the rest of the state, and strongly divided sentiments characterized its people during the Civil War. Guerrilla activities on behalf of both sides were regular occurrences here. In addition, Federal horsemen slashed through the area in repeated efforts to neutralize the Virginia and Tennessee (now Norfolk and Western) Railroad, which linked Virginia with Tennessee and the entire Western theatre of operations. This area became the leading source for some of the Confederacy's most necessary resources: salt for its citizens, coal for its naval vessels, and saltpeter for gunpowder. While few visible signs of the war remain today, this southwestern area offers the most scenic drives in Virginia.

Southwestern Virginia

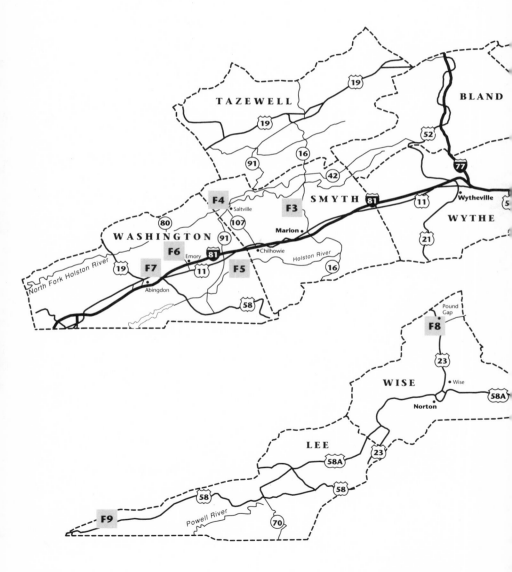

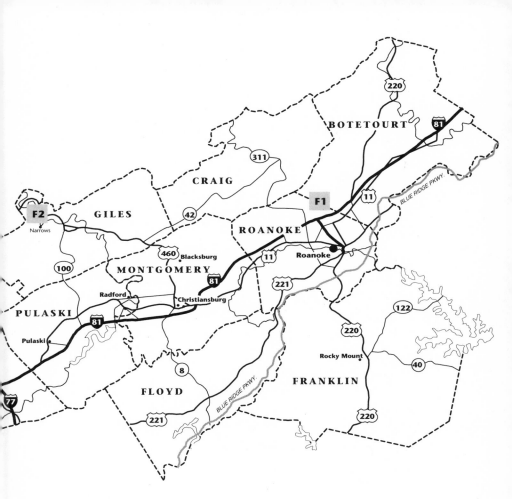

N

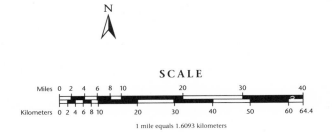

SCALE

Miles   0 2 4 6 8 10   20   30   40

Kilometers 0 2 4 6 8 10   20   30   40   50   60 64.4

1 mile equals 1.6093 kilometers

F1 HANGING ROCK A plain, triangular-shaped monument stands at the site of a June 21, 1864, running fight between Gen. David Hunter's Federal army, retreating westward from Lynchburg, and Gen. Jubal A. Early's pursuing Confederates. At the time of the war, Roanoke (then called Big Lick) was an insignificant village straddling the Virginia and Tennessee Railroad.

Leave I-81 at Exit 41 and drive northward on Virginia 311 for 0.4 mile. The historical marker is on the right-hand side of the highway, with Hanging Rock itself directly across the road.

F2 NARROWS This hamlet was one of the strategically important sites in southwestern Virginia. It is the most easily defended point along the vital New River (which, incidentally, is considered by many geologists to be second in age only to the Nile). Narrows remained in Federal hands until May 1864, when Confederates reoccupied the town and constructed a fort on the adjacent heights. Both sides used nearby, conspicuous East River Mountain as a signal station.

Present-day U.S. 460 passes through the narrows formed by the New River.

F3 MARION An 1838 schoolhouse building is the setting for the Smyth County Historical Museum, where may be seen scores of artifacts—including a bullet-riddled Bible that saved the life of a Confederate soldier.

The museum is at 230 N. Church Street.

F4 SALTVILLE Much of the common salt for the Confederacy came from this remote village. Its salt wells were of extreme importance to the embattled South. Confederates beat back a Federal attack here in October

1864; but two months later, Union forces seized and destroyed the works. The wartime wells no longer exist, but brine ponds and the hills where fighting occurred remain.

At Chilhowie (Exit 13 on I-81), proceed north on Virginia 107 for 8 miles to Saltville.

F5 OLD GLADE SPRING PRESBYTERIAN CEMETERY Situated behind a church established in 1772, this cemetery has the remains of Gen. William E. ("Grumble") Jones, who was killed in the 1864 battle of Piedmont, and Dr. William L. Dunn, a surgeon with Mosby's Rangers.

Leave I-81 at Exit 11, proceed east a short distance to U.S. 11, then south for 0.2 mile.

F6 EMORY Many Confederate soldiers, either prostrate from illness or wounded in fighting at nearby Saltville, were brought here for treatment. An Emory and Henry College building served as a hospital. Just west of the campus, on a hill overlooking the small community, 206 soldiers lie buried. A stone and bronze obelisk contains the names of all but two of the Confederates.

From Exit 10 on I-81, drive west on County 737 and bear right at the railroad tracks into Emory. Near the downtown, turn left on County 866 for 1 block, then left again between the second and third houses to enter the cemetery driveway.

F7 ABINGDON This was an important railroad depot and supply base during the war. In 1862 townspeople contributed all of the church bells to the Confederacy for melting into cannon. At different times, Confederate Gens. John Hunt Morgan and John C. Breckinridge used Abingdon as headquarters. Federal troops captured the town in December 1864 and set fire to a number of the main dwellings.

Martha Washington Inn   Still in use as a hotel, and almost identical to its Civil War appearance, this large inn served as a military hospital for much of the conflict.

It is on the south side of Main Street, directly across from the world-famous Barter Theater.

Confederate Marker   In Sinking Spring Cemetery is a walled-in area containing a large tombstone to "Unknown Confederate Dead." The exact number of Southern soldiers buried here is not known. However, the burial plot originated in September 1861 when 17 Louisiana soldiers were killed in a train wreck on the edge of town.

The cemetery is located one block north of W. Main Street on Alternate U.S. 58 West.

F8   POUND GAP   One of the few avenues through the rugged mountains of extreme southwestern Virginia, this spot was the scene of two skirmishes and two brisk engagements fought for control of the pass. Future President James A. Garfield commanded Federal troops in one of the actions. In December 1864 Union forces permanently secured the gap, then burned the county courthouse and 20 homes in nearby Gladesville (now Wise). Vestiges of earthworks are said to exist in the woods on either side of the mountain pass.

Pound Gap is on U.S. 23 at the Virginia-Kentucky border.

F9   CUMBERLAND GAP   Six times during the war, opposing forces skirmished over possession of this vital gateway between the Eastern and Western theaters of war. Today only a roadside historical marker calls attention to Cumberland Gap's Civil War history. Yet a dazzling view from its heights offers moving proof of the strategic importance this site had during the sectional conflict.

Cumberland Gap is on U.S. 58 at the Virginia-Kentucky border.

Index